416B

PEERS, P[...]
AND PHE[...]

C000320067

PEERS, PEASANTS AND PHEASANTS

Judy Vowles

FARMING PRESS

First published 1996

Copyright © 1996 Judy Vowles

All rights reserved. No parts of this
publication may be reproduced, stored in
a retrieval system, or transmitted, in any
form or by any means, electronic, mechanical,
photocopying, recording or otherwise, without
prior permission of Farming Press Books & Videos

ISBN 0 85236 325 7

A catalogue record for this book is available
from the British Library

**Published by Farming Press Books
Miller Freeman Professional Ltd
Wharfedale Road, Ipswich IP1 4LG, United Kingdom**

Distributed in North America
by Diamond Farm Enterprises,
Box 537, Alexandria Bay, NY 13607, USA

Cover design and illustration by Andrew Thistlethwaite
Typeset by Galleon Typesetting, Ipswich
Printed and bound in Great Britain by Biddles Ltd,
Guildford and King's Lynn

Chapter One

'AND there are stones in the show paddock,' declared his Lordship darkly, fixing John with an accusing eye. 'We don't want one of the best horses going lame.'

There was no sensible answer to that. His Lordship's Stud was situated upon 50 acres of chalk and flint, there were stones in all the paddocks. My husband nodded.

'Well, we must get rid of them,' went on our employer decisively. 'We will pick them up. I shall come on Saturday afternoon and we will move them. It shouldn't take long if there are three of us.' That being the end of the matter, his Lordship pulled shut the door of his Mercedes with a quietly expensive click, started the engine and drove with great dignity from the yard. John and I looked at each other. Still in the first month of our new job, we had quickly come to expect these little whimsical ideas from our employer. 'Not an easy man to work for,' agreed the locals, who had mostly been born and raised in the employ of his Lordship. 'Heart in the right place, mind, but – well, just not easy.'

We walked slowly back across the show paddock to the little cottage that came with John's job as manager of his Lordship's Stud. It had been another long day, starting at 7.00 am when the stock were turned out into paddocks, followed by a morning cleaning boxes. A brief lunch, then back to halter train young stock and school them to the disciplines expected of them in the showring as representatives of his Lordship's stables. John kicked at a flint moodily. The prospect of spending what might have been a free

I

Saturday afternoon stone picking was not a happy one. The weather had been unusually dry in April, belying the stories of April showers that John had heard in his native Africa. The small flints just below the chalky soil of the paddock were brought easily to the surface by the horses as they cantered and trotted around, showing their paces to his Lordship's guests. If we spent the whole of Saturday picking them up there would be twice as many more lurking beneath – just waiting.

The cottage welcomed us, the warmth of its kitchen driving away the chill of the early spring evening. The kettle sang cheerily on the hotplate of the battered old Rayburn, and in its oven the big cast iron casserole bubbled. For John and I it was a second marriage, with a cumulative bonus of five ready-made children, four boys and a girl. At each end of the scale were Mark, 13, and John, 19, both of whom were away during term time but zoomed home for holidays. The

three at home, Richard, 17, James, 15 and Joanna, 14, were a willing workforce when directed by John, whose African farming upbringing had given him a good grounding in the organisation of labour. So when the 'old fogeys', as they disrespectfully called us, crawled home at night it was always to find supper cooking, tea in the making and the happy atmosphere of home. The umpteenth-hand furniture had been brought home from the salerooms in the back of the horsebox after an enthusiastic spending spree that had filled the house for a few pounds. Nothing matched, except in condition – which was terminal – but it didn't matter. The cottage welcomed us: like chicks under the wing of a brooding hen we gathered together each evening in the warmth and comfort of her being.

The village of Woodford could well have been beamed down from above, a present to south-west England from that Great Architect in the sky. A narrow road snaked across the open downlands, rounded a hill, dropped steeply into a valley and suddenly it was there, a little cluster of white, thatched cottages around a thirteenth-century church. The howling, blustery winds that flew unhindered across the downs ignored them completely, nestling cosily in the lea of the hill, and came shrieking past to batter the windows of our little cottage perched high above the village. Behind the ancient church, thick woodland thrown protectively around it like an old shawl, stood the Manor House. And inside, more often than not, rattling around like a medium sized pea in a gigantic pod, would be his Lordship. Rattling around with him were Thomas and Maisie, a brave man and wife team who buttled and housekept for our eccentric employer with that wonderful, diplomatic firmness for which the British butler is famed. And secure in their care, his Lordship ruled his Estates and Woodford with the same good-natured arrogance as his father, grandfather, and great-grandfather had done. Woodford belonged to his Lordship, and so did its inhabitants.

To the left of the church lived Bert, his Lordship's gardener. His wife, Maggie, 'did' for his Lordship, and their son, Peter, was apprenticed to Walter, his Lordship's gamekeeper. Walter lived in the cottage beyond the Manor Wood, where he could keep an eye on his rearing pens and the rest of the village. His wife, Lillian, looked after his Lordship's chickens and fed the peacocks. To the right of the church another thatched and whitewashed cottage housed Jim, the dairyman, whose ancient dung-spattered Land Rover took him off at 4.00 am each morning to milk single handed the Estate's 150 cow dairy herd, and woe betide anyone who met him on the narrow road coming home to supper at 7.00 in the evening.

Across the valley from us, looking at Woodford from the other direction, sat another little cottage, one up two down, where Mac, his Lordship's shepherd, lived with a pack of collies and some very fast cats.

The other seven or eight dwellings in Woodford housed

a slowly changing population of tractor drivers, forestry workers, assistant stockmen, general farm workers and, of course, Mrs Stone, widow of one of his Lordship's previous gamekeepers.

A tiny village shop was pressed into Mrs Stone's front room, where one could find anything from a pound of onions to a pair of pants, a new broom or a packet of seeds. A kind, sympathetic lady, Mrs Stone would accept a down payment of 50 pence on a pair of warm gloves and 10 pence a week at nil per cent interest. Her finger was kept firmly on the pulse of Woodford's little community and, on the five square feet of linoleum across the counter from Mrs Stone, many were the problems solved, judgements made and reputations discussed. It took a smart one to get past Mrs Stone.

And on the hill looking down on the village and adjoining our cottage was his Lordship's Arabian Stud. Fifty acres of post and railed paddocks surrounded a neat stable complex of twenty looseboxes built around a courtyard with a clock tower and pigeon loft. The horses, fifteen brood mares, five stallions and assorted progeny, were proudly shown and expensively pampered by his Lordship, and deeply loved and managed by John, my husband. Also on the love side came Jane and Debbie, the two girl grooms, and myself, a willing dogsbody. Hi, I'm Judy.

Bert, his Lordship's gardener, dropped in to see us the next morning. 'Thought, seein' it's Saturday, y'might like t'come on over this afternoon an' pick out a few plants for this wilderness y'call a garden,' he grinned, waving an arm at the colourful carpet of bluebells, daisies, dandelions and docks that crept within a yard of the back door. 'I got some good strong plants comin' on, both flowers and vegetables, I shan't use 'em all.'

'Bert, that would be really great, and thanks for the offer, but we're working this afternoon.' John scowled out of the window in the direction of the paddock. 'We've been invited to join his Lordship in a stone picking party.'

Bert's grin deepened. 'No! Really? His Lordship picking stones?'

'Come on in, Bert.' I swept my daughter's school books from our one guest chair and cleared the breakfast dishes from the table in front of it. We had slept late that morning, making it a mid-morning breakfast by the time we had finished our usual stable chores.

'Glass of cider?'

'Well, Missus,' he glanced at his pocket watch and then tucked it quickly away beneath the folds of his many pull-overs, 'that'd be nice. I'm not in too much of a hurry. If y'can't be a bit leisurely on yer day off, when can you?'

'Exactly,' muttered John.

I found a tumbler, a wine glass and a mug and fetched the cider from the cold marble slab in the larder. We would have to get some proper glasses, although there was little room in our budget for such luxuries.

Bert took up his drink and pulled the chair a bit nearer to the warmth of the Rayburn. 'Bit cooler than you're used to, I reckon?' He raised bushy, greying eyebrows in Brian's direction and took a sip from his glass. 'Lot 'otter in Zimbwe . . . Zim, well, Rhodesia really, ain't it!'

'Well, it gets pretty cold there at times,' remarked John, 'and then it gets pretty hot as well. The difference is you know when it's going to do which.'

'That's useful,' agreed Bert, 'You bin there Missus?'

'Not me Bert, I'm a Pom.'

'Webbed feet come as standard,' explained my husband, seriously.

Bert was studying his glass. 'This i'nt real cider, y'know,' he commented at last, carefully placing it on the kitchen table with a gently suppressed hiccup. ' 'Tis too damned gazzy this commercial stuff. All very nice, an' thank'ee very much Missus, but,' he drew his chair closer in conspiratorial man-ner, 'I can tell 'ee where t'get the *real thing*.' Interest showed immediately on my husband's face as he leaned forward to join the huddle and catch the whispered words.

'Westnoll,' breathed Bert, casting a swift glance over his shoulder to the open kitchen window, where the pale spring sunshine filtered in. 'Mr Mills, Westnoll. Anyone there'll tell 'ee where t'find 'im.'

The name didn't mean much to us.

'Well,' explained Bert, ' 'tis only little. You 'as to want t'go there t'go there, if y'see what I means. Don't lead nowhere else. I'll draw 'ee a little map – is this 'ere rubbish?' He carefully tore a strip of card from the top of an empty cornflakes packet and with the thin edge of a carpenter's pencil dug from his pocket, he began to sketch out the route.

'Through Barfield and down the 'ill. Past three oak trees in a clump, and the next turning right. There's always a Jersey cow in the corner field there,' and he solemnly marked the cow with a cross. 'Then y'just follow yer nose till y'get to the pub and ask anyone for Joe Mills.' He pressed the rough sketch into John's hand with a knowing little wink, picked up his coat and began to pull on his wellies at the door. 'An' I tell 'ee what,' Bert puffed as he hauled determinedly at his snug-fitting boot, 'if you'd bring us back a pint of 'is medium brew I'd deem it a favour.' He slipped quickly through the back door, to avoid letting in too much cold air, and nodded his farewell. 'Be seein' you then. Remember me to Joe when y'see 'im. Oh, and 'appy stone pickin'!'

When he had gone John studied the map closely. 'Well,' he remarked thoughtfully, 'looks pretty straightforward, as long as nobody moves that cow. Perhaps we could go tomorrow, it'll be a nice excuse to explore that area anyway.'

At 2.00 pm precisely his Lordship's Range Rover drew into the neatly swept yard of the Stud. In suitably casual clothes, well-fitted green wellingtons and gardening gloves, his Lordship was obviously ready to head the team, and at 2.10, armed with skips from the stables and the largest wheelbarrow, we sallied forth. The rest of the family had all become deeply involved with homework at lunchtime, so unfortunately had to withhold their willing assistance, but I had to hand it to his Lordship – he could certainly pull his weight. Stones into skip, skip into wheelbarrow, stones into skip, skip into wheelbarrow. John caught my eye and grinned. 'If we could only get him singing,' he whispered, tipping his skip noisily into the barrow, 'it would be just like home.'

John and his employer took turns to empty the wheelbarrow into a large heap at the side of the lane, to be collected later by a tractor and trailer, as slowly and systematically we worked our way across the little field. By 3.30 I noticed that his Lordship was beginning to be more selective in his choice of stones. Only those from hens' egg size upwards seemed worth collecting and we were swift to follow his lead. By 4.00 we had progressed to goose eggs and were covering the ground much more quickly, and by 4.30 we reached the hedge at the far side of the paddock. Easing an aching back I noticed with some admiration that his Lordship still seemed fresh as a daisy, as he peeled off his green-thumbed gloves and looked back across the paddock in satisfaction.

'You see,' he addressed us solemnly, 'just a couple of hours and we have completely cleared this area of dangerous flints. Not a lot of effort needed, not a lot of time, just a systematic and sensible approach to the problem.'

We nodded and muttered in dutiful agreement.

'A cup of tea?' suggested John, quickly. We were standing beside the gate leading into the cottage garden.

'Ah . . . thank you, no.' His Lordship turned away and glanced swiftly at his watch. 'I have guests coming this evening. Now, tomorrow,' he paused, 'no, unfortunately I have to be away tomorrow. First thing on Monday, then, I would like to see how the foals are leading. We must practise seriously now for their first shows.' Then with a brief 'Good night', he left us.

'Phew,' John opened the little gate for me and followed me

through, 'for a minute there I thought we were going to lose Sunday too.'

Indoors Joanna and the boys had managed to finish all their homework and were well into a serious game of Monopoly. As usual, James was in the lead, closely pressed by Richard, while Joanna argued. I pushed the kettle over onto the hotplate to boil and began to gather warm towels from the rail of the Rayburn.

'You make the tea, I'll run the bath,' suggested John.

'OK.' I handed him the towels.

'Oh.' James noticed us for the first time. 'How did the chain-gang go?'

'Fine, how was the homework?'

'Fine.'

'I made a refrigerator stew.' Richard carefully stacked his money out of James's reach. 'It's in the oven.'

'How do you mean, *refrigerator* stew?'

'Everything he could find in the fridge,' explained my daughter.

'All the left-overs, and there were a few sausages, I chucked them in too. It'll be good, you'll be surprised.'

I was constantly surprised by the practical and warm-hearted support from these sons of John. I smiled and endeavoured to look enthusiastic. 'I'm sure it will be. Do we have time for a bath?'

'Of course.'

I poured us all a cup of tea.

'Bath's ready,' yelled John from upstairs.

Bathtime had become a pleasant ritual. Besides the obvious saving in time and hot water, it was usually the only really relaxing time of the day, and it was natural for us to share it. For John, sitting on the plug with the bathtaps dripping down his back, it looked fairly uncomfortable but, as he pointed out, I did a very good job in raising the water level and, besides, where else was there to put the soap? A cloud of steam escaped as I slipped through the door and dropped my

9

gown and towels over the rickety white painted chair.

'Come on, man, it'll be cold.'

I handed him his cup of tea. I was getting used to being called 'man'. I undressed quickly in the unheated room, and eased myself gently into water so deliciously hot that I could feel the goose pimples racing up over my shoulders and away. Like the steam, warmth and peace enveloped us as we sipped our tea and swapped memories of the day, progressing naturally to memories of the past. We had so many to trade, coming as we did from such different worlds.

I was, as John put it, a Pom. Not a very good Pom, though, for as he pointed out, my generally laid-back and fatalistic attitude towards life was not far removed from the primitive. 'You'd be happy in a mud hut,' was my husband's usual comment when I waved aside our total lack of 'necessities' like two sets of sheets each or a wardrobe of vaguely matching clothes. However, good or bad, I was English, though as a child my father had instilled in me his own interest in and fascination for Africa. It was strange how we had lived almost parallel lives. In my teens I would take my pony and ride out all day alone across the New Forest. Often I would sit quietly in the saddle, letting him graze slowly up to within yards of the wild deer. I would follow faint trails, ford streams and watch kingfishers, meet the gypsies, ride among the herds of wild ponies, search for mushrooms and ride home with pockets bulging with chestnuts. At the same time, in Africa, John was sitting quietly astride his horse, letting it graze up to herds of kudu. He would ride alone through the bush, meeting the local Africans in their villages and sharing their hospitality. He chased warthogs, trying to grab their sticky-up tails, and was chased back and treed by wild pig.

As the bath water cooled we topped it up again and John told me more of home – the land, the animals and the people he'd loved and had left behind. He only hinted at the sadness, the terrible war that had torn apart the land that would always be his home. With his family to think of he had made the only decision. When we had met, such a short time ago, it had been as if we had each found the other half of ourselves. We were kindred spirits, of that there was no doubt, and with my fascination for Africa and John's deep longing for his home I couldn't help but feel that God had a future planned for us.

At last the hot water ran cold, and Richard's yell of 'Supper – come and get it!' brought us tactfully, if abruptly, back to the present. The stew was really good. It was actually just a thick, chunky vegetable soup with strips of smoky bacon and sausage rings. With the locally baked crusty bread and the apple pie I had hidden to follow, who could have wished for more?

'So, who's coming to look for farmhouse cider tomorrow?' asked my husband as we sat drinking our bedtime cocoa, and watching the last glowing sticks of the fire turn to grey.

'Well, I was going for a ride.' Joanna looked hopefully at her stepfather. Encouraged by John she had quickly formed a very good relationship with the only gelding at the Stud, a quiet and beautifully behaved Arab of mature years.

'Fine,' nodded John, and raised an enquiring eyebrow in the boys' direction.

James shook his head. 'No thanks, Dad.'

'You two go,' said Richard firmly. 'It's not really our scene.' Then he grinned. We both knew what he meant. We were being let out on our own. As things turned out, it may not have been one of his wiser moves.

Chapter Two

SINCE our arrival on the Estate in January we had found little time to explore. Finding the job had been one of those slim, outside chances that went a long way towards proving that somewhere things had been very carefully planned. It had been a casual remark from a secretary in the estate agent's office while home hunting. She had an Arab mare, she had told us, and it was hopefully in foal to a rather special stallion. Always drawn towards horses, especially Arabians, John soon had the Stud's address and telephone number, and without a second thought casually rang his Lordship and suggested that he might like to show him around. Surprisingly, he had agreed. It just so happened that his Lordship's Stud manager was leaving so, unknown to John, the visit had taken the form of an informal interview. Before returning home his Lordship had offered John the job. It had been incredible – suddenly we had a new home, a new job, and with our new marriage came a new beginning.

So Sunday morning saw us bowling down the narrow winding lanes towards Westnoll. It was the second week in May, and the hazel coppices were bursting into their first early leaf, standing ankle deep in thick carpets of bluebells, which made the air heavy with their fragrance. In the warm, bright, early spring sunshine the ancient little Renault seemed to find new life too as she fairly zinged up the hills, staggering a bit towards the top and then catching her breath before zooming down into the valleys. Bert's map was on my knee and I traced the spidery lines with a finger as we followed the route he had given us.

'There are the three oak trees.' John nodded towards them as we passed. 'Should be next on the right. Watch out for a Jersey cow.' As we approached the turning a small brown, black and gold cow grazing in the corner paddock lifted her head and watched us out of dark, liquid eyes as we passed.

'There she is!' John craned his neck to see over the hedge, narrowly missing the ditch as he did so. 'What comes next?'

Bert's map was a bit like a treasure hunt . . . find three trees and a Jersey cow, then . . . 'Turn right by the Traveller's Rest, and better ask the first person we see.'

The first person we met along the lane turned out to be a sprightly old lady walking a portly spaniel on a lead. 'Joe Mills? Yes, he's just through the village and out the other side.' She waved a hand vaguely. 'You can't miss it, an old thatched cottage, stands alone in an overgrown garden.' She smiled and raised a querying eyebrow. 'Cider?' Then, nodding knowingly, she continued on her way.

'Britain's best-kept secret,' grinned John, waving our thanks as we passed.

'Westnoll' proclaimed the lichen-covered, hand-painted sign proudly as it lay half buried in the thick grass and nettles that verged the winding lane. 'Please drive carefully through our village.' On each side of the road the ancient trees, oak, beech and chestnut, were beginning to awaken once more to yet another year. Children on bicycles stopped and stared and then waved cheerfully.

'That's got to be it!' The brakes of the little Renault squeaked protestingly as John drew to a halt by a half-open gate. From there a path had been beaten through the dense tangle of grass and weeds to an old thatched farm cottage, with whitewashed walls and diamond window panes. It was overhung by centuries-old oak trees, the branches of which served as choirstalls for a multitude of birds. Spring flowers fought for survival among the young stinging nettles, and blackbirds squabbled noisily in the elder bushes, but there were no orchards to be seen. As we picked our way along the path to the front door, mice squeaked and scuttled through the dead leaves beneath the beech hedge and bumble bees hummed loudly in the primroses. The last hundred years had passed unnoticed here. John knocked loudly and from somewhere deep inside we heard footsteps. The door opened, and there before us stood Mr Mills.

The man himself could have stepped right out of the sepia prints my grandmother kept on the piano in her front room. Five feet high and spherical, his ancient black trousers were held up by some tired-looking braces, backed up by a wide leather belt which strained gamely at the last hole. His white shirt was open to reveal a grey hairy chest, while his head was completely bald and weatherbeaten to a deep, freckled brown. The round smiling face folded and crinkled around a pair of bright, twinkling grey eyes, and his feet and trousers were thrust into heavy black boots, laced up in a hit and miss fashion, with large knots at intervals. He needed only to take up the old hand-worn holly staff, which leaned against the wall behind him, to complete the picture.

Mr Mills beamed an answer to our tentative query. 'Cider? Oh ye-es, that's right, s'right, s'right, a-ah . . .' The voice tailed off as the head nodded vigorously in agreement. 'Would 'ee like t'try zum?' He closed the door carefully behind him. ''Tis around 'ere if 'ee'd like t'cum round. 'Ave 'ee cum far?'

'Woodford Estate,' answered John. 'Do you know Bert Williams?'

'Bert Williams?' echoed Mr Mills, and his smile grew broader, 'God luv us, yes! Bert and me went to school together. Well,' he paused and chuckled, 'when we went, that is. I 'spect it'd be nearer the truth t'say we used to miss school together. Yes, that's more like it.' His face lit up with memories, and he began to nod once more, 'Aye, that's right, s'right, s'right, s'right, a-ah . . .'

We followed him around the side of the house to a big,

black wooden shed, and stood back while Joe swung open the heavy doors. In the darkness we could just make out the shapes of three enormous barrels and an old cider press. As our eyes became accustomed to the gloom I noticed that an aged, chipped cup sat on top of each barrel. Joe Mills bowed to me.

'Sweet, medium or dry, Ma'am?'

'Oh, medium I think, please.'

Taking the cup from the central barrel he turned it upside down and gave it a brisk smack, peering inside doubtfully before drawing off a cupful of thickish brown liquid. He handed it to me with a flourish, reminiscent of the vineyards of France.

'An' the Gen'leman?'

'I'd like to try the dry, please,' decided John.

Mr Mills agreed with his choice. 'Very good this year,' he confided, exploring the inside of another cup with a stubby forefinger before topping it up from a second barrel. My husband clinked cups with me solemnly and we drank the health of Mr Mills.

Cool, semi-sweet and viscous, the first draught slid innocuously over the tonsils, leaving a sharp but not unpleasant taste of apple. The second swallow went straight for the throat. The sour roughness of it attacked with a ferocity that took my breath away and made my eyes stream. Trying desperately to breathe normally, to smile and not cry, I quickly swapped cups with John, and as I took a desperate gulp I saw, too late, the warning in my husband's eyes. Only a connoisseur could have distinguished the dry from the vinegar.

'Too dry?' The old man looked concerned as I began to cough and, hastily grabbing another cup, he poured out a generous measure of the sweet to balance things out. Just to be fair, John was given a brimming cupful too, and Mr Mills settled happily back to watch us drink. I wiped my eyes, blew my nose bravely and sipped the thick, sweet brew. 'Delicious,' I smiled back at Joe. I was never going to finish it, somehow

15

he just had to be distracted. John must have tuned into my thought waves. By Joe's feet lay a dusty three-legged stool.

'Just the thing,' exclaimed my husband, grasping my arm and pointing to the stool. 'Just the thing for milking your goat.'

'Oh?' Mr Mills looked interested, ''Av 'ee got a goat then?' He bent down to pick up the stool and our cider instantly disappeared among the stinging nettles around the door post behind us.

'Well, no,' I confessed, 'not yet. But I would like one.'

'Yes,' agreed John, returning his empty cup to the top of the 'sweet' barrel, 'we've both always wanted one.'

'Well now,' puffed Joe – bending was obviously an effort for him – 'my neighbour's got two for sale.' He began to rummage through a box of bottles, looking for some with tops. 'When 'ee've decided which cider 'ee'd like, I'll take 'ee over there.' He glanced at the empty cups. 'Liked the sweet best, did 'ee then? 'Ow many pints would 'ee like?'

To give credibility to the way we had knocked back the samples, we settled on four pints of the sweet and a couple of the medium for Bert, for which we were charged such a modest price that it didn't seem to matter that we wouldn't be able to actually drink it. Joe followed us out to the car where we stacked away the assortment of recycled bottles, then led the way across the road to another old cottage. This one had a slate roof and a well-kept front garden behind the neatly clipped hedge. Its owner was around the back, digging busily, as we were shown through the little wicket gate at the side, and down the path to be introduced as 'a lady and gen'leman very interested in your goats, Dan'l.'

Daniel jammed his fork into the ground, wiped his hands carefully on the seat of his trousers and greeted us warmly.

'I'll leave you good folk to talk business, then,' suggested Joe. 'I'll be seein' 'ee again, no doubt?'

'Yes, yes,' declared John, 'we'll be back, now that we've found you.'

The old man's face crinkled into a delighted grin. He drew closer to lay a hand on my arm. 'Plenty more where that cum from,' he assured us in a confidential whisper. 'Plenty more! All 'ee 'as t'do is ask,' and, waving away our expressions of gratitude, he headed off up the garden without a backward glance.

Daniel was a brisk, cheerful-looking man in his sixties, with a brown face and kind, gentle eyes. He pointed to part of the lawn which had been roped off to accommodate a shaggy little pony.

'That's why the goats have got to go,' he explained. 'Grandchildren wanted 'im and we haven't got room for everything.'

We wandered with him down towards a garden shed behind some currant bushes. 'We've had them shut up and I've been cartin' grass to them, but it takes up so much time, I just can't manage it all. I wouldn't want anything for them, to be honest I'd just be happy for them to go to a good home.'

He pulled back the bolt and two goats skittered out into the sunshine. We knew nothing about goats, but one immediately caught our attention. From the moment we saw her we just knew that this goat was ours! She was basically white, long legged with a slightly roman nose and ears which stuck out rather like handle bars. Her eyes were big, bright and grey, with long lashes, and her face was a pale, almost mushroom brown with a white centre stripe. There was another large patch of brown on her back.

'She's Anglo-Nubian cross Saanen,' Daniel announced proudly, and then threw in for good measure, 'and her grandmother was Toggenburg.'

We gazed at her.

'She's in kid,' Daniel was saying. 'Don't rightly know what the billy was 'cause my son took her, but she's due in June.'

John looked at me quizzically, and read my thoughts. 'You're quite mad,' he shook his head, 'quite mad. Where on earth would we put her?'

'Well, we've got a big enough garden, and no one has time to plant anything.'

'That's true,' agreed my husband. 'So you think we should convert the weeds to milk?'

'Absolutely.'

John sighed. 'You've made up your mind, haven't you!' I could see that he was hoping I had.

'It really is a good idea.' I went along with trying to convince him, as he shook his head doubtfully, trying his best not to look delighted.

'Well, of course, it's absolutely crazy, but' – he turned to Daniel who had been standing quietly watching us with an understanding twinkle in his eyes – 'it rather looks as if we would like to offer her a good home, Daniel.'

I hugged him as Daniel, beaming with pleasure, went off in search of a 'bit o' binder twine' for a temporary collar. In no time at all the back seat of the little Renault had been folded up and a bed of straw put down, and after a few encouraging shoves and heaves our goat was induced to climb aboard. Once in the car and on our way she seemed happy to enjoy the ride, gazing with interest at the passing countryside, and twisting her head around for a second look at some grazing sheep. Clasping our bottles of undrinkable cider I glanced at John and saw that he had the same big happy grin on his face as I did. 'Quite mad,' he was muttering blissfully to himself, 'go to buy cider and come back with a goat!'

'What will the children say?'

'Heaven knows.'

The children, still wary from their experience of having young stinging nettles served up as spinach for Sunday lunch, were unlikely to be enthusiastic. As we made our way lazily homewards I looked out across the beautiful spring countryside. The beech trees were in full delicate leaf and the wild flowers were opening their petals wide to the warm sunshine. Beneath the trees the little copses shimmered in a haze of brilliant, vibrant blue. John breathed deeply, taking in the wonderfully blended perfume of flowers and trees, the very essence of spring. 'Now that's a good name for a goat!' he exclaimed suddenly.

'What?'

'Bluebell. Well, cows used to be called names like Daisy and Honeysuckle, didn't they? Why not a goat called Bluebell?'

I turned to our goat. 'What do you think?' She gazed solemnly back at me.

My husband peered at her in the driver's mirror. 'She likes it,' he confirmed decisively, 'she just winked.'

The children accepted Bluebell's arrival as being generally in character with the nuttiness they had come to expect of their parents. Surprisingly little comment was made. Joanna loved all animals, could understand our impulsive action, and was ready to go along with our first attempt at self-sufficiency. James mildly pointed out that none of us had ever tasted goats' milk, and that he for one had no intention of doing so. Richard was willing to be convinced, but we would have to be convincing.

Meanwhile, Bluebell settled down very well in her new surroundings, and took to the wilderness we called a garden as a duck to water. She soon had the area mapped out in her mind, and imposed her own boundaries, presumably related to the distance she felt safe from home. Luckily we had no near neighbours, as we quickly learned that fences and gates are no barrier to a healthy goat, and once we knew she could find her way back safely she was allowed to roam freely. At night she slept in part of what was originally a coal shed. We burned wood only in the kitchen Rayburn, so coal hadn't been stored in it for some time. We brushed it out and whitewashed the walls, and John built a wooden pen with a raised floor for her to sleep on, and bedded it deeply in straw. The door was always left open and she could come and go as she pleased, sometimes dozing during the day and foraging at night. The garden lost its overgrown look as the docks disappeared and left room for new grass to spring up, and hedges became trim as Bluebell munched her way through young hazel, ivy, beech and, to our consternation, lilac, currant bushes and the groceries from the back of the Renault.

As she got to know us better she became very much part of the family and precautions had to be taken to prevent a bloodless coup. She would wander into the house if the door was left open and was partial to sitting on top of the car if it was left in a position which suited her. She would creep into the back kitchen and raid the vegetable rack for carrots and apples, the same vegetables being left untouched when sliced and mixed with her feed. When she came to trust us enough to play I stole many a half hour away from my chores to join her in mock fights and chases. She would rear high on her hind legs, wheeling and shaking her head, to come down short of me with inches to spare. As she became heavier in kid she began to stay nearer the house, and our games became less exuberant. We had decided to keep at least one kid as company for Bluebell and to use the rest of the milk for the house, so with this in mind John made a second pen adjacent to Bluebell's, to separate her from the kids overnight so that there would be milk for us in the mornings.

As we had no idea of the expected kidding date we kept a very close eye on her as she grew larger and larger. With every passing day we felt it just impossible that she could hold back any longer, and each morning I would be up at first light and out to the little shed in dressing gown and slippers, to see if Bluebell had become a mum overnight. We were both secretly hoping that the unknown Billy had been Anglo-Nubian, although we realised the chances were pretty slim. Those wonderful long floppy ears always seemed to give them the kind of appeal rarely found beyond the world of Disney.

It was John who went down to make tea that morning. He looked at me sombrely as he placed the tray on the bedside table. 'I think you had better go and look in the goathouse,' he said quietly and then, as I leapt out of bed and grabbed my gown, he added, 'What sort of Billy has ears that do this?' And he placed a balled fist on either side of his head with the index fingers sticking bolt upright.

A goat with pricked ears? I galloped down the stairs, missing the last three steps completely to fall in an untidy heap while my gown, which I had neglected to do up in my haste, landed in a neat pile next to me. Painfully I limped out to the shed and peered around the corner. Bluebell was pulling hay from her rack and looking very smug, and there in the straw beside her stood two of the most beautiful little creatures I had ever seen. One was black with dark brown markings, rather like a bumblebee, the other was mushroom brown and white. Their fur was thick and soft. Big bright blue-grey eyes gazed at me steadily, and the pert little faces were framed by ears so long that they seemed in danger of tripping over them as they fought for balance on their new-found legs.

Suddenly I realised that my husband was standing next to me, wearing a grin from ear to ear. 'S'right,' he nodded, 's'right, s'right, s'right, a-ah!' Then: 'Boys or girls?'

I picked up Bumblebee. 'Girl!' I stroked the beautiful ears and she nibbled experimentally at my nose.

John picked up the other one and peered underneath. 'Girl!' he announced triumphantly, dropping her back in the straw hastily as she gave an ear-splitting yell for mother. I sat down in the corner and watched, enthralled by their absolute perfection. Both had found their way to the milk bar, and two little tails wagged furiously in time to the very satisfactory slurping noises, while Bluebell carefully inspected each little rump as they fed, making reassuring motherly noises as she did so. John came back with a bucket of warm water to which he had added some black treacle and salt, which our goat book had assured us would be gratefully received. Bluebell promptly tipped both kids over in the straw in her haste to get to the bucket.

'They're quite different.' John had been studying the kids closely. Apart from the obvious difference in colour, Bumblebee was much stockier than her sister, who was longer in the neck and legs and had a more pronounced roman nose. It gave her a distinctly Arabian look. Searching for something to combine this with 'Bluebell' we fell upon the unlikely name of Arabella. Arabella and Bumblebee!

The family appeared, half dressed and sleepy eyed to inspect the new arrivals.

'Oh!' Joanna knelt beside them. 'Oh, they're fantastic!'

'Super,' agreed Richard.

'I expect they'll drink a lot of milk,' James put in hopefully.

Chapter Three

IT was clearly going to be one of those days. I had just managed to light the Rayburn, which had been in a particularly stubborn mood that morning, and learned that a fire that devours three *Farmers Weekly*s, an armful of kindling and then goes out can still give you a very nasty burn. It was raining, and having eventually persuaded the fire to go and set the oven warming, I needed two more eggs to make the cake I had planned. There's nothing like freshly laid free-range eggs, if you can find them, and I mooched around the wet garden following faint trails and peering under bramble bushes with a mounting feeling of frustration, as the rain trickled down my neck and the wet grass stuck my trouser legs to my knees. Then the water seeped into the channels of the cord material and ran unhindered down the insides of my boots to slosh around my toes.

Had God made anything more stupid than a chicken? We provided warm, straw-lined nesting boxes, conveniently situated, dry and inviting – but did our chickens use them? Not they! I gently rubbed my wrist where a stinging nettle had got me. Egg collecting was a daily battle of wits between the chickens and me, and I was forced to admit to being frequently outwitted. As I stood there, trying to put myself in a chicken's place in choosing an unlikely nesting spot, I heard a tell-tale proud clucking coming from Bluebell's shed. Stealthily I approached. As usual the door was open wide. Bluebell and the kids lay snugly in the straw watching the rain drift past and there, high above them on a jutting shelf, only just visible in the darkest corner of the shed, perched the brown hen clucking smugly. She jumped as I appeared in the doorway and stretched her neck jerkily to follow my movements.

'So that's where you've been going!' I shook a finger at her. 'Why do you think I feed you, eh? It's give and take in this world, my girl.'

I looked around for something to stand on; I could probably reach from the edge of Bluebell's manger. The brown hen became more agitated as I approached, and rose to her feet, clucking in alarm. As I hauled myself up the wall she panicked and turning round swiftly she kicked the egg. As I went up I met the egg coming down. It bounced off my shoulder and I grabbed wildly for it with the expertise of a volleyball player, sending it zinging across the pen to hit the doorpost where it slid slowly and stickily into a heap at the bottom. The brown hen and I studied each other. Then, reading the murder in my eyes, she launched herself clumsily into the air, landed heavily outside the door and, squawking hysterically, disappeared down the wet garden at a bandy gallop, leaving me in a cloud of cobwebs, dust and feathers.

I sat down in the straw next to Bluebell and we watched the rain together in a philosophical silence. Pulling an unprotesting Bumblebee onto my lap and leaning comfortably against Bluebell, I resigned myself to fate. Who wanted a rich, dark, Dundee cake anyway, with all that fattening fruit and cherries, just a dash of brandy and roasted almonds. The wind shook the branches of the old beech tree, sending the accumulated raindrops earthwards in sudden heavy showers that drummed on the roof of the little shed. June! The kids were five days old, and next week, I had promised myself, we would begin to be even more self-supporting by adding goats' milk to the menu. To give weight to my decision I had cancelled the order we had with Bill, the milkman from the village. I shrugged deeper into my wet jacket and sniffed. It was all going to be so much healthier for us.

My watch showed 10.00 am and, with the idea of Dundee cake abandoned, I topped up the Rayburn and squelched my way across the paddock to the stables. It was the blacksmith's day, and John was always glad of an extra pair of hands. My finger still burned from the Rayburn's vicious attack, my wrist was smarting from nettle stings. Why not complete the hat trick and get stomped on by a horse!

I found John in the Stallion's box, talking quietly to him, while a pale but determined young man struggled to hold his balance and a hind foot as the horse, ears flat, repeatedly snatched it away. There were five other stallions at the Stud, but for John this one was special. Soon after our arrival he had been horrified to see this horse throw its handler to the ground and kneel on him. By the time he had managed to get the Stallion off the lad had been quite badly bitten, and from that moment my husband refused to allow anyone else to handle the horse. It was only then that we had learned of his reputation. Apparently he had bitten his handler badly in front of hundreds of onlookers in an international showring and several past members of the staff had scars to vouch for his ill temper and the speed with which he could strike. Debbie and Jane, who made up the rest of the full-time staff, were only too pleased to leave him to John – but then he saw the Stallion in a different light.

To my husband this was an animal that had never known sympathy or understanding, and in the six months that they had been together he had worked hard to tune into that defensive and suspicious mind. There had been no spark of friendliness in the Stallion's eye, just a cold, silent contempt, and proud aloofness from man, who in his youth had given him reason for submission, but no reason for respect. Now the girls and I would often sit on the top rail of the paddock, cowboy style, and watch them working together with a quiet understanding that was wonderful to see. John would set him free and then, by just talking to him, would have him walk, trot and canter around him in a circle as if on an invisible rein. Using just his voice he could stop him, change his direction and start again, and at the finish he would call him and walk away without a backward glance, and the Stallion would follow quietly at his shoulder. Between John and the Stallion a bond had been forged, but the rest of us were still treated with suspicion that was, admittedly, mutual.

A team of blacksmiths came to the stables: Ben, a master farrier, with several assistants and a lethargic apprentice known affectionately as Lightnin'. On arrival the first thing to be settled was always which poor unfortunate would be shoeing the Stallion. Then, this weighty decision made, the rest of the team – relief showing on every face – dispersed in various directions to deal with the other horses. I crept past the Stallion's box and that week's unhappy loser before I disturbed anyone's concentration, and picking up a headcollar from the tackroom went in search of someone to help.

From a three-year-old colt's box in the stallion line came a series of muffled thumps and scuffles. These were liberally spiced with some very descriptive and quite imaginative epithets which, I thought, could have been interpreted loosely as a request for help. As I appeared in the doorway Ben dropped the colt's foot and passed a heavily muscled arm across his red and sweating forehead, an exasperated expression on his usually placid face.

'Will you please come and stop this bloody animal from sitting on me!' he demanded irritably. The colt turned his beautiful head and looked innocently at me, but I knew exactly what he was up to. Passive resistance you could call it. He wouldn't snatch or be aggressive, he'd just slowly collapse on top of you until you had to let go.

I joined Ben in the box and gave the colt's neck a friendly slap. 'I think he'll behave if I stand by his head.' I had learned something about this colt. 'You see,' I added helpfully, 'he loves having his mane combed, he just goes into a trance.'

Ben, sweat dripping freely from the end of his nose, shot him a withering look. 'Bloody pansy,' he growled, 'an' if you can pick up a hind leg an' comb 'is mane that'll be a trick worth seein'.'

Unabashed I pulled a mane comb from the soggy tangle of binder twine, tissues and horse-nuts that filled the pockets of my wet jacket and started combing. The colt dropped his head to a more comfortable level, his eyelids drooped and he stood resting a hind leg, completely relaxed. As Ben lifted the foot experimentally, the colt sighed happily and lowered his head further so that the bit behind his ears could be reached. Ben shook his head, and his annoyance was replaced by a sarcastic smile.

''Oo's a pretty boy, then?' he teased. 'That reminds me.' He straightened up suddenly and stretched his neck to look out across the yard. 'Did you pass my dog on your way here?'

'Didn't see him.'

Ben was always accompanied by a scruffy little terrier who trotted innocently around looking for mice in the straw bales and stalking pigeons.

27

'Most expensive dog in England,' Ben remarked ruefully, as he rummaged in his tool box for a file. 'Keep yer eye on 'im, he'll kill anything. Cost me ninety quid last week.' He picked up a foot. 'Caught a parrot. Oo'd a thought e'd find a parrot – the bloke weren't 'alf mad. Ninety quid!' He shook his head and, as I watched, the dog pattered quietly past. 'If he weren't such a good excuse for gettin' out in the evenin's I wouldn't bovver wid 'im.' He sighed and gave the hoof a few strokes with the file. 'Week before it were 'alf a rabbit.'

'*Half* a rabbit?'

'All 'e could reach through the cage.'

I shuddered and changed the subject. 'How's Lightnin' coming along, then?'

'Oh, 'e'll do. Got 'im sum good bones this week.' He drew the colt's foreleg between his knees and examined the hoof closely, head on one side.

'Bones?' I asked, puzzled.

'Yeah. Every 'orse's foot 'as got bones in it, 'asn't it? You got t'understand the bones afore yer can understand the foot. Feet and leg bones. I got a good friend what works in the knacker's yard, and any 'orse what comes in wiv summat wrong wid 'is legs or feet 'e boils the bones down for me.' He picked up the final foot. 'I got sum real puzzlers at 'ome, amazin' what can 'appen to an 'orse's leg bones. I could bring 'em along if'n you're interested,' he offered generously.

'Oh, I would be,' I assured him. 'So you have to be a bit of a vet, too?'

'Yeah, well the vet'll often ask a good blacksmith's opinion. It's 'is job after all. 'Orse dealers, they come up wid a lot o' tricks. Did I tell yer about the 'orse wid a pea in its ear?'

'No! How did that happen?'

'Dealer put it there. Lazy old 'orse, y'see, couldn't make it look smart no how, nobody 'd buy it, so they come across this idea. Put a pea in its ear and it kept shakin' its 'ead and lookin' lively – could 'ear it y'see – give it summat t'think about. Then the people what bought it 'ad the vet t'see it, an' 'e found it.'

'How did they get it out?'

'They 'ad to wait for it t'sprout – dark in there so didn't take long.'

Well, I'd swallowed that one. Ben gave me a wicked sidelong grin and I was just about to have second thoughts about the half a rabbit story when the pale young man who had been shoeing the Stallion came in. Ben's glance took in the dishevelled appearance, the pallor, the shining eyes and bashful grin that spelt success. He nodded, 'All done then?'

'Yep!'

'Congratulations, lad. Pour yerself a cup o' tea then. I've just about finished with Petal 'ere.' He inclined his head towards the mesmerised colt. 'Then we'll go and 'ave a go at some of the mares.' He collected up his tools. 'Thanks for your help, Judy m'dear. Are y'comin' to the Show?'

'Yes,' I unbuckled the colt's headcollar, and he shook himself awake. 'John's showing the Stallion – I'd hate to miss that.'

The County Show was just a few weeks away, and very much a social occasion for everyone on the Estate. Those not actually involved with any livestock that his Lordship decided to show would be given the day off to go, and it was a very popular annual get-together. For John this Show had particular significance, for besides the two fillies that had been chosen to represent the Stud, his Lordship had agreed to allow John to show the Stallion. It was a time of testing, for although John knew that he had gained the great horse's confidence he had to prove to himself that it was strong enough to stand the tense atmosphere of the showring.

'Rather 'im than me,' Ben shook his head emphatically. 'I see'd what 'appened to the other chap. Took 'is finger right off yer know.'

I did know and was trying to forget it. 'Well,' I told him, 'I think this will be something really worth seeing.'

'Be worth seein',' agreed Ben. 'We're on the farrier's stand, givin' a demonstration and doin' emergency shoein'.' He turned to the younger man. 'I 'ope you got them Stallion's shoes on tight, Alan, 'cause that's a demonstration I wouldn't relish in front of fifty-odd people, all 'opin' for a disaster!'

Alan grinned. 'Be like 'is Lordship's own Show, be all accounts. I hear Mac's giving a demonstration too – sheep-dogs.'

'Well, we'll see you there then, m'dear. Let's pray for a bit better weather. Now where's that bloody dog disappeared to!' And, whistling hopefully, Ben and assistant made off in the direction of the mares' yard.

Chapter Four

MAC was his Lordship's senior shepherd, and had quickly become our very favourite character on the Estate. He was also our nearest neighbour, living on the hillside across the valley from the stables, where his little one-bedroomed cottage was surrounded by sweeping downlands and clumps of woodland. The garden had been completely taken over by a varied assortment of chickens and ducks, which seemed to live happily side by side with several generations of semi-wild cats. Here the law of nature prevailed, whereby the sheepdogs kept down the cats and the cats controlled the freely breeding fowl population. A dozen Chinese geese acted as watchdogs and it was their musical chorus which enabled Mac to have the kettle boiling for a welcome cup of tea by the time any visitor had made the steep climb up from the roadside gate. Mac was a Scotsman, with a hearty bellow of a voice and a leathery brown skin that came from over half a century of co-existence with his sheep in all the sun and rain, snow and gales that the British climate hurled at him. He never seemed to have less than six collies around, ranging from young pups ready to work through to his favourite working bitch and an amazingly agile three-legged dog which moved so fast that it was impossible to detect the disability until the animal was actually standing still. There was a highly lucrative sideline in selling trained sheepdogs, and over the years Mac had gained a very wide reputation for his ability to produce good dogs. I had always found it difficult to understand how their new owners managed, as all Mac's dogs responded to a mixture of broad Scots and Gaelic, which must have been extremely difficult for anyone else to follow.

Mac called in to inspect Bluebell and the kids, news of their arrival having spread as quickly as if I myself had given birth to twins, and he stood gazing at the little lop-eared creatures with a soft smile on his tough, weatherbeaten face. 'Och,' he said at last, dropping on one knee beside them, 'they're grand wee babbies.' And the gnarled old hands that must have helped hundreds of lambs into the world reached out to gently stroke their thick baby fur.

The old shepherd accepted my offer of tea, and we sat side by side in the sun and talked of his coming sheepdog demonstration. 'Aye, it gives me worms in ma stomach jes' thinkin' aboot it,' he confided gloomily. 'Och, ma dogs are fine, but ye know how it es, they're like bairns – however good ye know they are, when ye want them to show it they let ye doon. An' I dinna want t'let his Lordship doon, neither!'

I was sure he wouldn't. The sight of Mac bringing several hundred sheep in over the downs always made me stop in my tracks and watch. I would stand spellbound as the sheep poured like a white river over the lip of the horizon, flowing quickly and smoothly through the gateways and down into the lower pastures, controlled quite silently by the black flitting shadows of his dogs as they answered Mac's seemingly undecipherable calls.

He sighed. 'Och, weel, it'll be right I dare say. Aye, I'd rather be doin' that than leading that Stallion your good man's takin', and there's no mistake.' He drew a shiny new pipe from his pocket and, putting it between his teeth, began to shave wafers from a block of tobacco into the palm of his hand with a wicked-looking knife.

'Birthday present?' I suggested, noting the pipe. Mac usually smoked an ancient black one.

'Och, no. Ma good pipe had an accident. Aye, I was sortin'

lambs in the pens, and this ewe – by, she was wild – she caught me right behind ma knees. Aye, I sat down so hard I clean bit through the stem of ma pipe! I'll tell ye,' he chuckled in aftersight, 'the air was tartan!'

He stood up slowly and puffed with concentration until a glow appeared. 'Weel, thanks for the tea, Missus. I must be on ma way. I had a good ewe die this morning for no reason and the vet's comin' oot to do a post mortal.'

I walked with him to the gate, and stood as he climbed into his little car and wound down the window. 'See ye at the Show, if not before.' And with a cheery wave he coaxed the wheezy engine into consciousness and went clanking and rattling down the hill.

Left alone, I prepared myself for the afternoon milking session. Milking looked so easy. Obviously the milk was stored in the udder and let down through the teat, so all one had to do was squeeze the teat and – bingo. Not so! You had to hold the teat in such a way that the milk came down and not back up. And you had to hold your goat in such a way that you could hold the teat. It had taken days of trial and error before I had managed to work out a system. You put food in a bucket in the corner and jammed your goat's head into the bucket, which took care of that end, and then placed the milking bucket strategically in place. With your right shoulder and right temple you then pinned your goat against the wall and shoved your left leg straight out in front of you with the toe of your wellie pointing inwards, ready to stop the front end from swinging round. Then you sat on your right heel and grasped a teat firmly in each hand.

It was frequently necessary at this stage to pick oneself up from the straw, replace milking bucket and restrain goat with binder twine to door hinge. After a fair amount of milk had been spilt and a few frustrated tears shed, despite the old trite saying, I found it best to milk one teat at a time to start with, which gave me a spare hand to balance the bucket and keep Bluebell's feet out of it. Eventually I sort of got the knack of it. You squeezed the top of the teat between the base of your thumb and forefinger, effectively trapping the milk which was in the teat, then keeping that pressure you squeezed gently in a downwards direction without pulling, forcing the milk out and hopefully into the bucket. Then you did it again, and again, and again. After a while, when you were sure that your goat would stand still, you could do it with both hands alternately to produce a rhythm. It took some practice to get the speed right, and I was getting quite good at sitting in the Russian Cossack position. Considering we were both beginners, Bluebell had been very patient and had really only knocked the bucket over on a few occasions, usually in her efforts to flatten the odd chicken that sidled up to steal either her grain or some milk, to which chickens are very partial.

'There,' exclaimed John proudly at breakfast on one of those first mornings. 'Now we can have this filled to the top every day,' – and he lovingly placed the brimming half-gallon jug in the centre of the table. There wasn't a rush. James glared sulkily at it for a moment or two.

'I think I'll wait until Bill comes with the proper milk,' he decided.

'Bill isn't coming. I've cancelled the milk, I'm afraid it's this or nothing.' I heaped muesli into my bowl and poured a liberal amount of milk on top. 'Mmm,' I went on, helping myself to a bit more, 'delicious.'

'Just complements the muesli,' agreed John. 'It's got a real nutty flavour.'

'Would have,' muttered James sarcastically, pushing his bowl to one side.

'Actually, I'm not too hungry this morning. I think I'll just have eggs and bacon.'

'Black coffee?' I pushed a cup towards him.

He scowled. 'I don't think it's funny. I'm not drinking stinking goats' milk, and that's that!'

'Well, I'm going to try some,' decided Richard suddenly,

34

and taking a deep breath he gingerly tipped a few drops into his coffee and stirred in an extra spoonful of sugar. 'Helps the medicine go down,' he explained cheerfully.

Joanna finished her cereal up without comment.

Breakfast over and the children away to tackle homework, John voiced thoughts for us both. 'Has got an odd flavour, hasn't it. Do you think it's supposed to taste like that?'

'I don't know, I think we just have to forget what cows' milk tastes like and stop comparing it. Anyway, I'll stick it in custard and things like that, that might wean us on to it gradually.'

James stuck to his word until breakfast two days later, when I noticed him filling his cereal bowl and reaching for the big brown earthenware jug. He scraped the bowl clean and followed up with two cups of coffee. I smiled inwardly. Now that was a major step towards independence!

The kids were into everything, bouncing with good health and mischief, and it was obvious from their round little tummies and happy faces that Bluebell had milk to spare. In the days that followed we milked her each morning before letting the kids out, and again in the evening after they were tucked up contentedly in their pen. She gave us, on average, five pints a day, which we used in the house. With a large proportion of the milk we made curd cheese, yoghurt and a semi-soft cheese we had seen made in France. The whey went into baking, and the kitchen was filled with the delicious aroma of fresh bread and scones and home-made strawberry jam.

John was becoming more and more busy with the horses and it wasn't long before I found myself caught up in the general day-to-day work of the stables as well as helping on the special occasions. The kids ranged far and wide with Bluebell now, and could be suddenly encountered on any part of the Stud. His Lordship seemed not to notice them, and they were never mentioned, although to stare determinedly into the far distance as a goat investigates one's

trouser leg takes more than the normal amount of British reserve.

With twenty-five boxes to clean out every morning, and an equal number of horses to care for, we were all kept pretty busy, and time for such homely pursuits as cheese- and breadmaking became taken up elsewhere. Soon the fridge was filled with several days' milk standing in various containers, and mixed batches of cheese which were sitting dejectedly on the larder shelf, in pots shielded from flies by an old net curtain, were beginning to make their presence known.

It was as John watched me scrape the last of these failures into the chickens' bowl that an incredibly bright idea hit him. What we needed most in the world, right now, was a pig! The more he thought of the idea the greater his enthusiasm became. If we partitioned off part of the garden and borrowed an arc from Mac, the pig could live there. It would root up the garden, conveniently fertilising it at the same time, and we could feed it on the spare goats' milk and barley meal. The chickens would peck over the newly turned ground and eat up the insects and beetles, and we would then move them all on to the next part and plant vegetables. We would split the garden into three sections and the pig would move from the third section to the freezer in the form of pork and bacon.

Never one to let an idea grow cold, John spent the following weekend carefully fencing the garden into sections. Early Monday morning a large pig arc arrived on a trailer pulled by a tractor and John carried it into position by the simple method of getting inside, walking hunchbacked to the selected site, and collapsing. Mac, who had obviously had some experience with pigs, and had visions of them running amok through his Lordship's cornfields, had kindly sent some heavy metal hurdles to reinforce our new fence, and a trough or two. With all these exciting new additions to our garden it began to look positively forlorn *without* a pig, and I began to feel the first stirrings of interest, which up to now had been very, very dormant.

The goats immediately took over the pig arc, Bluebell investigating the inside and the kids leaping on and off the top in one of their endless games of tag. They were completely fearless and unbelievably nimble. They also had absolutely no respect for person or property. Just a few mornings earlier I had come downstairs after making beds, to start clearing away breakfast, and found Arabella curled up happily in the centre of the kitchen table. She was surrounded by glasses, plates, cups and jugs, which had been quite undisturbed, and she was peacefully dozing, completely oblivious to her surroundings. The peace was short lived when I found her, but she leapt gracefully to the floor and from there to the windowsill and away without so much as a spoon falling.

Visitors were now requested to leave their cars at the gate and walk in, as cloven hoofprints on the roof and bonnet of a beloved vehicle can quickly lose one friends, as we had found to our cost. Even the chickens were at risk, as Bumblebee had discovered that she could pick them up by the tail feathers when they had their heads down in their feed bowl.

As usually goes with country folk, a friend of ours had a

friend who had a sow, which just happened to have a large litter of piglets ready for weaning. 'Perhaps we should wait until after the Show,' I suggested practically. The great day was less than a week away, and I had a feeling that we would have enough on our minds without the added excitement of a pig in residence.

Chapter Five

A T his Lordship's stables, preparing an Arabian horse for a show was as painstaking as preparing a beautiful film star for her first major appearance. As in all beauty routines, the basics were a healthy diet and regular controlled exercise, which gave correct shape to the body and condition to the skin and coat. This was a long-term operation, and began as soon as the foal was weaned. The final preening usually took us two days.

On day one came the trimming, of which we all whole-heartedly disapproved. To present a clear fine outline of the head to the judge, all the fine hairs around the muzzle, which are normally used much as a cat uses its whiskers, were shaved off. The protective fur inside the sensitive ears was clipped away and any unwanted hair around the fetlocks removed. The rest of the day was spent polishing show bridles, washing rugs and bandages, making lists and checking everything. The horsebox was bedded down with deep straw and all the showing kit stowed away for a quick start.

Day two was shampoo day. Jane and Debbie dealt with the two fillies and I helped John with the Stallion. While gallons of water heated up in the big coppers, the four of us busily gathered together buckets and sponges, brushes and scrapers, combs, shampoo, conditioner and towels. The sky looked ominous and there had been a few heavy showers during the night and previous day, so the whole operation was carried out in well-scrubbed looseboxes.

Securely tied, the big silver Stallion stood quietly as his

coat was thoroughly brushed to remove as much loose hair as possible. He shifted a little as the warm water was sponged over him, sinking through the coat, wetting his skin and running in grey rivulets down his face. Taking a side each we massaged the shampoo to a good lather and, using a very soft brush, worked it well into the coat. John dealt with the mane, which was too near the teeth for my liking, and the tail, which was also situated in a danger zone. Next came the first rinse, and we staggered back and forth with brimming buckets of clear warm water, liberally sloshing it over our feet and each other as well as the Stallion, and scraping the remaining lather away with rubber scrapers. Then a second and third shampoo, until the rinsing water came away absolutely clean.

I had persuaded Mrs Stone, who seemed able to provide anything, to get us a gallon of hair conditioner from her wholesaler, and a cupped handful of this was worked into the long, shoulder-length mane. Tangles fell away miraculously before the comb as the cream did its work, and the tail received the same treatment. Another bucket of warm water to remove the surplus, and a final gentle pat with towels. The Stallion accepted it all without protest. John took him off for a walk around the yards to dry off while I collected together his rugs and bandages which were to keep him clean until the final unveiling. They both came trotting back, running before a storm which was already throwing plump raindrops against the tackroom windows; the Stallion shook his head proudly, tossing the gleaming mane as if he fully appreciated the beautiful picture he made against the gathering black clouds.

We had decided to travel that evening and stay overnight at the showground so that we would have plenty of time for last-minute preparations in the morning. Richard was left in charge, taking a couple of days off school without too many signs of regret, and Joanna had happily taken over the task of goat milking before and after school. Fitting the two yearling fillies into the same horsebox as the Stallion took a bit of organising, but at last they were all aboard and we were on our way. Jane and Debbie travelled ahead in the Stud car to sort out the stabling and their own overnight accommodation. His Lordship was to arrive at the Show the next day, in time to take one of the fillies into her class.

The weather hadn't improved, and we drove through sunshine and showers, with leaden skies forming a perfect backcloth for the soft clear colours of the occasional rainbows, which materialised and faded as we drove along the narrow puddled lanes and out on to the broad main highway. Two stables had been booked at the showground for the fillies, but John had felt it would be unsafe to leave the Stallion in one of the rather flimsy temporary boxes, so he was to stay in half of the horsebox and we were to turn the other half into our living quarters so that we could be close on hand. The journey went relatively quickly, and the route was well signposted as we neared the showground, meeting more and more boxes and trailers, until at last we were in a queue of show traffic making for the exhibitors' entrance.

Progress was slow then, and it wasn't until the box in front of us moved through the entrance that we realised why. The showground had obviously had more than its fair share of heavy rain, and the big lorries had turned the whole parking area into a quagmire. It was impossible to drive through, and each lorry was being hitched up in turn to a relay of powerful tractors to be towed to a parking spot and dumped. As we were left in our allotted space John and I looked at each other. The showring, we knew, was at the other side of the vast show complex, the mud was over a foot deep – and we had on board a gleaming white horse.

We jumped messily down from the cab, and after quickly checking that the horses were all calm and happy we sloshed our way in the general direction of the stables, slipping and sliding at each step as the mud sucked at our boots and holding on to one another for support. Once away from the lorry park the ground was much better, as the walkways through the permanent showground were hard surfaced, and at last we located Jane and Debbie in our stable block, tucked away behind the sheep stands and cattle houses.

'Bugger,' said John quietly. He stared into space for a few moments. 'We're going to have our lorry, equipment and the Stallion at one end of the showground, and the fillies at the other. For crying in a bucket, it's impossible, man!'

He marched away to take stock of the situation, and was soon beckoning to us from the end of the horse lines. Debbie grinned. 'I think he's cracked it.'

When we caught up with him, he pointed: 'Look, it'd fit in there, wouldn't it?' A very convenient lorry-sized space had been left between the sheep and cattle areas.

'Well, yes – but I shouldn't think they'd let you . . .' I started to say, but my husband had already gone, and ten minutes later I was only mildly surprised to see our horsebox approaching, being towed into place by an obliging tractor driver.

'Just act as if we've every right to be here, and no one will question it,' whispered John.

Feeling much happier, we settled the fillies into their boxes, tucked the Stallion up for the night and then set about sorting out our living quarters. The half of the box which had been occupied by the two fillies was carefully bedded down again with fresh, clean straw. On top of this were laid our sleeping bags, pillows and blankets, and hey presto our bedroom was ready. The other compartment held our cases and provisions, a camping stove, kettle and frying pan. Jane and Debbie, yawning after the day's exertions, took their leave and made for their less primitive sleeping quarters and supper, while I prepared ours.

Our pre-Show meal was always the same and always welcome. Corned beef hash! Before long the unmistakable aroma of frying onions surrounded the box as they sizzled gently in the big pan. The Stallion pulled hay from his net and munched contentedly, watching the whole procedure over the top of his stall with ears pricked. Perhaps generations ago his maternal ancestors had shared their master's tent: he seemed relaxed and to be enjoying our company. He jumped a little as the tinned potatoes hissed into the hot pan, then blew noisily through his nostrils and returned to his own supper. When the onions and potatoes were a golden brown the cubed corned beef was mixed in and everything turned over and over until it was all piping hot. Thick wedges of fresh crusty brown bread, bought still hot from Mrs Stone's that morning, were spread liberally with butter and piled on a communal plate. The frying pan was placed between us on the straw bale bench, and with a fork each and a very strict line drawn down the middle it all disappeared as quickly as snow in summer. A man-sized mug of drinking chocolate rounded things off.

Toothbrushes were found and one tube of toothpaste. 'I'll give you a squeeze at the door of the Ladies,' offered John generously. I accepted. The showground was still busy as latecomers put up their stands and organised themselves for an early start, and we wandered in search of our nearest washrooms. Then, warm, snug and contented, we crawled into our soft straw-cushioned bed, to drift off to sleep lulled by the quiet sounds of sheep and cattle settling down for the night.

We were wakened very abruptly by a deafening screech that was alarmingly close and frighteningly hostile. The whole box rocked violently as the Stallion threw himself against the walls, screaming a furious and ear-splitting challenge, over and over again. It was just light, and John had already thrown his clothes on and leapt out of the box while I was hopping around with one leg in my jeans. We had parked alongside an area which was used by the stockmen to wash down the show cattle. It was equipped with cold running water and hitching rails and was, it seemed, just the place for the heavy horse handlers to clear the mud off the thickly feathered legs of the big draught horses. Through the vents in the side of the box the Stallion had a perfect grandstand view of these big docile creatures that had dared to invade his territory. Our fifteen hands of seething fury had no doubts as to his supremacy over these eighteen hand plus adversaries, whose handlers were casting sidelong glances at the bulging sides of the box.

John came back with a bucket of feed and a fresh haynet, but the Stallion wouldn't be distracted and kept up the tirade until the last broad rump disappeared around the corner. Then, peace miraculously restored, the Stallion tossed his head in satisfaction and allowed himself to become interested in breakfast. I couldn't help wondering what would happen if he won his class and was asked to join them in the Grand Parade, and I guess the same thought wasn't far from John's mind.

The next few hours were spent helping the girls get the fillies ready for their class and this was the part of showing which I enjoyed most. After their feed we took them for a short walk around the showground to acclimatise them to all the different sights and scents and sounds. Apart from being shown as foals with their mothers, this was their first real introduction to the showring. Already the hot-dog stands were stoking up and the air was heavy with the strange mingled smells of onions and fresh doughnuts, sweet hay, trodden grass, horses, frying bacon, leather, sheep, coffee and cows. A fresh breeze whipped them all up together and wafted them past the flaring nostrils of the little prancing fillies. It flapped the flags and tent sides, making them jump and sidestep, their tails high across their backs, snorting the hollow echoing alarm call of their wild ancestors. Occasionally they paid us the compliment of a little nuzzle to reassure themselves that they were in safe hands, as they gazed wide eyed in wonder at that strange new world.

Back in their boxes we collected together the paraphernalia of the equine beauty kit: soft brushes, combs, my inevitable lump of raw sheep's wool to give a final polish, hoof oil, mascara, greasepaint, hairspray, baby oil, chalk and

Vaseline. As before, the finished result relied strongly on a thorough basic grooming. The coat was brushed and polished until it gleamed and the mane and tail thoroughly combed out and baby oil brushed in sparingly. Their faces were washed with a damp sponge and Vaseline smeared over the muzzle and beneath the eyes to bring out the natural dark colouring of the Arab. Then, on these areas, the darkness was accentuated with a light touch of black greasepaint. Any white markings were picked out with chalk to make them whiter than white, and a final puff of hairspray from a top London fashion house kept the mane from blowing onto the wrong side of the neck. The end result, even from close quarters, was stunning. We were just thinking that we had earned some breakfast when Debbie popped her head over the half-door.

'Stand by,' she hissed. 'Here comes his Lordship.'

Jane ducked around the box gathering the scattered brushes and quickly tucked away a long strand of dark hair that had escaped from its band. Her pretty face was streaked with Vaseline and the odd smudge of greasepaint. Debbie wiped her hands on the seat of her jeans and nervously flicked an imaginary speck from her filly's neck. His Lordship had that effect on most of us except John, who, indifferent to class, treated everyone the same in his quiet, forthright way.

A tall, impressive figure, I always had the feeling that our employer moved inside his own invisible forcefield. I could hear him, see him, speak to him, but there was an almost tangible wall between us, and I was never comfortable in his presence. His very bearing forbade easy, informal conversation, and as he appeared a respectful hush descended. He nodded briefly to John and looked the fillies over critically. His Lordship had many years of showing experience behind him, and knew a good many tricks in the art of preparation and showing of his favourite breed. Usually his last-minute visit to the stable block produced a valuable tip or two.

45

'Yes,' he remarked at last, 'very nice. But I think we can improve on this one.'

He handed his hat to John, who passed it on to Jane.

'A little more shade here,' he indicated the precise spot as Jane hastened to follow his instructions, 'and here.' He studied the result closely and then nodded briskly. 'And more Vaseline here.' Jane wiped blackened fingers on a tissue as Debbie quickly handed her the jar. His Lordship took a final long, hard look at his handiwork and allowed himself a quick smile of satisfaction.

'Yes, yes. That's better.' And the filly was led out, tossing her head and prancing, so that we could all see the overall effect. It takes only a subtle change of light or shade to make the difference between a picture and a masterpiece, and in two minutes his Lordship had done just that. I stood there gazing at her, at the beautiful dished face, the big glowing eyes and flared, delicately curved nostrils. She held her head proudly, and the breeze rippled her chestnut mane as the sun appeared from behind the banking clouds to add its own final touch of gold.

I felt a nudge as Debbie sidled up, her hands behind her back. Something was passed to me with expressions of great secrecy and as I quietly slipped back into the box I found to my horror that I was holding his Lordship's hat – covered in mud and flat as a pancake. Jane had put it on the ground while she made those last-minute touches and, unnoticed by us, the filly had put her foot squarely on it. My first thought was to lose it permanently, but that would focus blame on Jane. Frantically I pummelled it back into shape and, keeping a nervous eye on the half-open door, I grabbed a dandy brush and gave it a vigorous scrub, which got rid of the surface mud. Luckily it was brown, so what was left behind blended in fairly well. The little feather looked a bit sad – bristles on end like a scared cat. I spat on a finger and tried to flatten it down, then pushed it further into the hatband. It would have to do; I could hear his

Lordship making ready to leave. Casually I wandered out and passed the hat to John who, in all innocence, handed it to his Lordship. He absent-mindedly placed it on his head while studying his watch. 'Their class is in twenty minutes,' he was saying. 'I would like you to be in the collecting ring five minutes before it starts.'

He turned and walked away, a tall immaculate figure. Expensive suit, gloves, silk tie and gleaming shoes. Only the hoof print on the back of his hat spoiled the picture.

John sprinted back to the horsebox to change and check the Stallion and then, looking exceedingly smart, he led one filly and Debbie led the other to the ringside. Here Debbie handed the rein over to his Lordship, and, with a suitable lapse of time between them to make the most impact from their entrance, they trotted into the ring. The quality of his Lordship's stock was very high, and it was almost a foregone conclusion that they would both be in the first five places, but the girls and I always enjoyed a personal bet on whether John or his Lordship would take in the winner. That time I lost out to Debbie, with his Lordship taking first place and John coming third. His face expressionless, our employer tossed the rein back to Debbie as he left the ring and, with a curt reminder that the winning youngster would be needed again for the final parade, he left us.

Jane was furious. 'You'd think he'd wish you luck with the Stallion, at least.'

John was unruffled. 'Luck doesn't come into it,' he explained. 'His Lordship needs to know he'll win, and I think it highly probable that we won't. The Stallion's being shown for me this time, and I'm grateful to him for that. Go on, take the fillies back, rug them up and go and see some of the Show, you've earned it.'

'Sure you can manage?' queried Debbie, giving her winning filly an illegal Polo mint.

'Sure, no problem. See you both after the Stallion class.'

'Good luck,' said Jane firmly, over her shoulder, as together

47

they led the fillies away, ribbons fluttering gaily from their bridles.

John glanced at his watch. 'Quick cup of tea and a sandwich,' he suggested. The Stallion's class would be in an hour's time and there was still a great deal of preparation to be done. Back at the box we brewed tea, made a pile of sandwiches and ate them, sitting side by side on the straw bale bench, watching the world go by.

I had always loved Agricultural Shows. At a show the best of everything that meant most to us came together in the one place. The expressions on the faces of the passers-by were as diverse as the exhibits. Pride mingled shyly with hope and anxiety. Happiness shone from the eyes of those whose triumph had been longed for but unexpected. Disappointment and sometimes bitterness from those who felt their defeat ill-deserved. Undisguised joy in old friends meeting once more, perhaps their one annual get-together. Toddlers, hanging grimly on to balloons and sticky candyfloss, stared bewildered and open-mouthed from their pushchairs at the kaleidoscopic scene around them. White-coated stockmen in well-scrubbed wellies led amazingly docile-looking bulls through the pressing crowds with as little concern as granny walking her poodle, while visiting townsfolk stood bravely within feet of the powerful beasts, showing just how plucky they could be. Queues of people marked the position of the ice-cream sellers and the hot-dog stands, and clustered around the umbrella-topped tables outside the beer-tent, the clink of glasses and bursts of laughter mingled with the strident tones of the very determined silver band. The sun had come out to stay and its warmth and brightness accentuated the happy mood of the occasion.

'Right!' Brian drained his cup and stood up, reaching for the Stallion's grooming kit and headcollar. 'Time we were getting ready.'

In the close confines of the box there was little I could do except stand like a theatre nurse handing things as required.

As with the fillies the procedure was the same, and soon the white coat gleamed and the magnificent flowing mane shimmered silver in the sun's rays. Once more the dark areas were darkened in a way that emphasised the size and beauty of the big bright eyes and the wide, curving nostrils. The show bridle John had chosen was of the narrowest plain rolled leather, and its daintiness gave emphasis to the power and fire of the proud animal it controlled. The Stallion seemed relaxed and unaffected by the sounds around him. Certainly he was no stranger to the showring, but he was reacting in a very encouraging way, without any sign of the tension that we had expected. As he was finally led down the ramp and through the crowds the mass parted before him like the waves of the Red Sea. He glanced around him with interest, arching his neck and stepping out, with his tail carried high in the characteristic manner of the Arab. I followed a few yards behind, trying to keep the general public from pushing babies in pushchairs under his back legs, and flinching as a friendly admirer gave him a hearty slap across the rump in passing. But this was a Show, and the Stallion's whole attitude had changed, seeming oblivious to the close proximity of the crowd as he moved towards the ring. His nostrils were wide as he took in the messages passed to him on the breeze, and his ears – forever mobile – deciphered the jumble of sounds which came to him from all sides.

Jane and Debbie joined us at the entrance to the collecting ring, where several competing stallions were already assembled. His pace quickened to a jog when he saw them, and the slim leather bridle and narrow chain linking the bit to the rein John held suddenly looked alarmingly inadequate as the Stallion weighed up his opponents, tossing his head impatiently against the restraint and half rearing onto his hind legs. His ears flicked occasionally towards John as he listened to the quiet reassuring voice he knew and suddenly the air vibrated with his challenge, causing those people pressed around the entrance to move aside hastily as he swept into the small ring. Two or three yards more and he went up, rearing high into the air as John expertly flicked the rein aside to avoid the striking forelegs. He came down to swing around, clearing a wide circle about him so that he stood alone and splendid.

' 'Struth, I wouldn't be 'im,' muttered a quiet voice at my side, and there was Ben wearing his familiar farrier's apron and a worried expression. 'Left Alan in charge,' he explained quickly, not taking his eyes off the ring. 'Couldn't miss this.'

At the far side of the ring stood an imposing dark chestnut stallion. His coat reflected the sunlight with an iridescent copper sheen and he stood calmly, taking in the scene before him with the confidence of a seasoned show animal. Jane and I glanced at each other. Here was the opposition. There might just as well have been no other animal in the ring, we both knew that the contest would be between these two.

As they began to file into the main ring before the judge the Stallion settled down and, remembering the lessons taught him by this man he trusted, he did as he was bid, standing correctly to present a good line to the judge and trotting out with the beautiful light floating action for which his breed is famed. For what seemed a lifetime the judge deliberated, conferred, walked around the Stallion and then around the chestnut. He stood at the side, then in front, and then had them both trot away from him a second time. Debbie, her freckled face frowning with concentration, was absent-mindedly tearing her programme into little strips. Jane gently took it away from her. The watching crowds, caught up in the tenseness of the moment, were strangely silent, each heart willing the judge to pick the animal that they themselves had chosen.

'Get on wiv it,' agonised Ben.

There was a sudden explosion of applause as the judge gave his decision, bringing the chestnut in to stand at the head of the line and motioning John to come in second. His smile and quiet remark indicated that the decision hadn't been easy. The Stallion accepted the blue ribbon on his bridle with the same impassiveness with which he accepted the deafening applause of the crowd as he was trotted past the grandstand on his lap of honour. Somehow his cold, aloof beauty created a special aura and for them it was a scene to remember and enjoy. For his Lordship, wherever he may have been, it was just another second, but for the Stallion and John it was an unquestionable victory.

People around us looked on understandingly as Ben, Jane, Debbie and myself hugged each other jubilantly, until at last John came through the onlookers, a delighted smile on his face, the Stallion jogging beside him on a relaxed rein. Together we formed a rear guard and followed them back to the horsebox, where we found Bert and several of his Lordship's staff waiting to offer their congratulations. Then, the Stallion tucked up happily with a special celebration feed, we all drifted towards the ring again for the next major attraction, Mac's demonstration.

The sheepdog demonstration was a new addition to the annual programme and a lot of interest had been raised by the 'One Man and his Dog' series on television. Suddenly everyone was an expert on sheepdog trials.

At the far end of the main ring stood a little trailer in which the sheep waited impatiently for their freedom.

At the end nearest to us a post had been driven into the ground and this was where Mac was to stand while his dogs put the sheep around and through the various gates and fences that had been temporarily borrowed from the show-jumping course. We settled ourselves on the grass below the ropes of the ring to watch as Mac's lonely form detached itself from the crowd. With two dogs closely at heel and a young one on a piece of string, he marched determinedly into the arena. He looked so smart! Mac's working gear relied very heavily on good darning, reliable patching and several lengths of binder twine in assorted colours. Now, in the ring, the Sunday best trousers were paired with a lovely tweed jacket and a hat set at a jaunty angle. He carried a beautifully carved crook, and his shoes gleamed brilliantly, despite the mud and wet grass. The loudspeakers whined and crackled into life.

'Now, Ladies and Gentlemen. The event we have all been waiting for, our local expert Mr McKenzie with his fine pair of working sheepdogs. Here to give us all a demonstration today of the real working relationship and understanding that this man has with his dogs.'

The audience burst into an enthusiastic round of hand-clapping and then an excited hush descended as someone let down the ramp of the trailer and six wild-looking sheep jumped out onto the grass. Firm at his post, Mac squared his shoulders, took a good grip on his crook and murmured something to Sweep on his right which sent him speeding away down the side of the ring. Before the dog was half way, however, the sheep spotted him. The lead ewe stamped a foot bravely, and the others gathered behind her presenting a bold front. Sweep, sensing an element of defiance in the air,

slowed down to a cautious stalking crawl, while Mac – sensing trouble – yelled something in Gaelic which may or may not have been misinterpreted by Sweep. His reaction was swift, however, and straight as an arrow he shot towards the sheep, who in turn – their confidence shattered – whirled around and headed in a body for the spectators. Clearly they regarded people as being a lot less hazardous than the lethal black shape bearing down on them, and men, women and children scattered in all directions as the little flock charged through the midst of the crowd.

Mac's instructions, as he leapt frantically up and down at his post, were partially drowned in the uproar, so Sweep used his initiative. Skidding past the sheep he sent them swinging back towards the ring, but by now they were really shunting along and Mac watched helplessly as they passed through the ring and out the other side, causing a fresh commotion. In desperation the old shepherd sent in the little bitch, and she – with Mac's commands still ringing in her ears – managed to overtake the sheep and turn them. Unfortunately, by the time she had done this their direct route back towards Mac lay straight through the barbeque pit, which they and both dogs took without check, scattering people, charcoal and beefburgers as they passed. This time they approached the ring from a different angle, meeting the same spectators and pinning them against the ropes. One man, who obviously didn't understand sheep, made the mistake of trying to stop the leading ewe, who caught him squarely on the knees, while the rest of the bunch passed over him.

Back in the ring the dogs finally gained control, and the sheep – panting but still defiant – were taken smoothly around the course in a way which delighted the unscathed portions of the crowd, who evidently reckoned they'd got their money's worth in excitement, disaster and entertainment. Mac had thrown down the jaunty hat at the height of his fury, and his wispy white hair shone like a halo around his balding head as he coaxed the last sheep into the little pen and slammed the gate on them. A gentle sigh of relief rose from the audience followed immediately by a wild clapping, whistling and cheering as Mac gave a solemn little bow and, with the three dogs jumping excitedly around him, vanished through the exit nearest the beer-tent.

Chapter Six

OUR prospective piglet's mother was a Large White, but I really had no idea just how large Large was until we faced her over the door of the sty. She was enormous, levering herself up on the inside of the partition to squint shortsightedly down upon us. There seemed to be at least fifty fat little piglets bombing about in all directions and cannoning into each other in the adjoining pen, and Dave, their proud owner, waded in and pointed out the ones he thought best. We were quite happy to go along with his choice – after all he was the expert – and in a sudden flurry of straw, squeals and muck he emerged clasping a very indignant and audible little pig in his arms.

'How's he going to travel?' puffed Dave.

John and I looked at each other. I suppose I had vaguely thought of having him on my lap, but I certainly couldn't cope with that furiously wriggling little monster. For one thing piglets are bald, there's nothing to hang on to, and for another thing the excitement was having an adverse effect on his bowels. Cuddly he was not.

'No problem,' grinned Dave, and grabbing a hessian sack he stuffed the defiant little piglet inside and tied the top with binder twine, finishing with a neat bow. 'There he is, snug as a bug in a rug.'

He set the sack down on the ground and it stood there, grunting suspiciously. It took a few experimental steps and grunted again. There was something very pathetic about that little sack. We left it there while we settled up the financial side of the transaction and came back a few minutes later to see that the sack was sitting down and snuffling quietly. John scooped him up gently. 'Poor sad sack,' he commiserated, and popped him into the back of the Renault.

Back at the stables we carried Sadsac into his new home and tipped him out at the entrance of the pig arc where, with a short bark, he shot through the door and buried himself right under the straw. The goats all came to investigate, sniffing the air, the sack and us with wrinkled noses and curious expressions, but Sadsac had clearly had enough excitement for one day and was in no mood to make another public appearance.

Next morning John and I leaned on the fence in the manner of all true stockmen, watching our pig slurping away happily at the thick gruel of barley meal and warm goats' milk. His face was half immersed in the porridge and it was disappearing in long sucks and gulps at an alarming rate, while his little pink tummy got tauter and tauter. In a sudden panic he realised that it was all gone and desperately explored every corner of the trough, shoving his snout underneath and flipping it over in a last hopeful gesture. Then, satisfied that nothing had been missed, he tottered away, rolling slightly, to bury himself in the straw again until lunchtime.

The brown hen came strutting up importantly to squeeze through the gate and peck hopefully at any tiny remaining specks in the trough. She was closely followed by her foster children, three beautifully speckled grey Marans. I don't know why we called her the brown hen, the dozen chickens we had were all brown, but she did have an especially deep chestnut sheen to her plumage and was by far the greatest character. She had insisted on going broody that spring, and as we didn't have a cockerel I had indulged in a little business deal with Maisie, his Lordship's housekeeper. His Lordship had a flock of the most handsome Marans, presided over by a proud and elegant cockerel. They were, of course, of impeccable breeding! Our chickens were laying well, so one morning I had gone to the kitchen door of the Manor House clasping a box of one dozen fresh eggs and suggested to Maisie that no harm would be done to his Lordship's digestion if twelve new-laid eggs were swopped for another twelve new-laid eggs. She had readily agreed, and a few minutes later I was trotting up the hill, triumphantly hugging my prize of one dozen dark chocolate brown eggs, which hopefully were fertile. The brown hen was delighted and sat tightly to her task, but with limited success. The cockerel, it seemed, had been all crow and little action. Nine of the eggs were useless, but she did hatch three fluffy little bundles of which she was justly proud. They had grown rapidly, and were now almost as big as their mother, but still cheeping and following in her footsteps.

Sunday was our only day of relaxation, and even then there were a few tasks to be dealt with. The horses were a seven day a week commitment, and there was always the early morning feeding and turning out to be done before everyone could relax and get on with their own personal projects.

My own personal project was Husham. Unless the colts born at the Stud showed particular promise they were gelded before they were a year old and sold on as prospective riding horses. Husham had been quite a promising youngster, but the decision was made not to keep him entire when he was a two-year-old, which meant he had a great deal of the fire and presence found in a stallion coupled with a beautiful temperament and a deep quiet intelligence. He was then three, and his Lordship had decided that he would like to have him ridden and had offered me the opportunity of backing and gently riding him. I had accepted the offer with mixed feelings of pride and panic. As a two-year-old he had earned the reputation of being very hard to handle. I loved to watch him cantering around the paddocks, his tail high over his back and his head moving from side to side as he took in his surroundings, shying and spooking at nothing and covering the ground with an incredibly light and airy movement. He was just bursting with the simple pleasure of being alive. He was so beautiful he sent shivers down my spine, but the thought of actually being on his back just about paralysed me.

I had never been a 'professional' horsewoman. I had a deep love for horses and usually seemed able to communicate with them, but I wasn't a good rider in the accepted sense and had never had a riding lesson. My childhood and teens were spent in the New Forest, where for the hard-earned sum of thirty pounds I had purchased a three-year-old New Forest gelding. He was caught straight off the Forest by a group of men who drove the whole herd into a cattle trailer, roped and tied him, then drove the rest of the herd out. Understandably he was very difficult to box after that. He was never 'broken'. We made friends, learned the basics of brakes and steering and within a fortnight were roaming the Forest, sometimes together, sometimes separately. Not being able to afford a saddle as well as a pony I learned to ride the hard way. If I came off I was liable to spend two days walking the Forest trying to find the herd he had joined. It was easier to stay on. I lost him four times and found him again, and each time unbelievably he allowed me to catch him and lead him away from the rest. In time I learned to stay with him whatever he did, and had him for eighteen happy years.

Husham, however, was no New Forest pony. His mother and father were National Champions and he was a hot-blooded chestnut.

'Get to know each other,' John had said in his calm reassuring way. 'Go for walks.'

So every summer evening and Sunday afternoon, Husham and I would go for a walk. We explored the fields and downs together, ducked through hazel coppices and hopped ditches. We met sheep and dairy cows, and pheasants and hares that jumped out from under our feet. We stopped and talked to the tractor drivers who kept their engines running while we chatted and fed Husham on jam sandwiches and pieces of fruit cake. We called on Mac and his pack of dogs and sat in the sun drinking tea, while the dogs sniffed around the horse's heels and yapped. We talked to donkeys over the fence, other riders on strange horses, and watched the deer leaping away from us through the woods. Before I ever attempted to get on his back Husham had met everything he was likely to meet within two miles of home and was completely confident. He knew all the words he needed to know, such as walk, trot, back-up and stand, and did them automatically. He would stop at the lightest pressure on his halter, and move on at a word. He was used to being rugged in winter, so the saddle and girth he took in his stride. Backing him was a very unremarkable event, he seemed not to notice my weight, and the fact that the voice came from a different direction didn't bother him. The words were the same and he reacted in his usual manner. Two ropes clipped to his headcollar acted as bridle and again the slightest pressure stopped him. We were on our way.

Our walks had become longer and we explored new ground together. He walked, trotted and cantered to word of mouth and the leg aids were introduced almost imperceptibly until he responded to either. When we were sure that he understood the messages passed to him through his rope reins we introduced a rubber bit, but again the transition was so gradual that he took to it without seeming to notice the difference. We went on long rides over the downs and up and down the steep hills that surrounded us, and Husham began to develop his muscles as well as his mind. He would never panic. He would stop and look hard at anything that bothered him, then walk quietly on. He didn't buck once during the whole time I was riding him, listened attentively to every word spoken and enjoyed our rides together as much as I did. Because he understood what was expected of him he did it of his own free will, and riding him did nothing to take away his spirit and joy of life. Sometimes John would saddle up one of the stallions and come with me. Then the pace tended to be a bit faster, as John's riding was far, far better than mine, and Husham would stand and stare, eyes popping, as they cantered joyously in and out of trees and rounded up stray sheep with loud whoops that excited and delighted the stallion and would have given his Lordship apoplexy if he had seen them!

Often our rides would combine pleasure with work. The sheep were frequently moved to remote parts of the Estate to clear up wasted grass after the cattle, or to trim the more unproductive parts of the downlands. Mac was always grateful for a check on these little far-flung groups, because sheep are notoriously accident prone and will usually wait until after the shepherd has been around before hanging themselves in hayracks or breaking a leg in a rabbit hole. As most of my favourite rides took me past his cottage and handling pens I was often asked if I would mind 'Jest seein' if ye can coont forty on their feet below yon far doon.' Husham enjoyed these missions too, for I'm sure he could sense when we were riding out with a purpose rather than just ambling.

One day Mac asked me to check on some store lambs in the grounds of his Lordship's Manor, where they were grazing down the rougher parts of the parkland. A temporary electric fence had been strung up within the park boundaries, dividing it roughly into North End and South End. I could see that North End had been grazed right down almost to the roots and the lambs were now in South End and tucking in eagerly. As I rode along the fenceline I noticed that a couple of them had somehow got themselves on the wrong side of the netting, and were trotting up and down anxiously, trying to get back with the rest.

The fence was activated by a New Zealand type of energiser, which I knew from experience gave you a pretty hefty zonk if you touched the wire. I also knew that Mac's free and easy approach to the maintenance of his fencing equipment meant that I wasn't going to touch anything with much less than a bargepole. Mac had had so many shocks over the years that he was practically immune to electricity, and I once watched him hold an electrified wire while shaking hands with a lady visitor, making her practically leap out of her shoes. So, followed by a very puzzled Husham, I crawled around the fencing unit on my hands and knees trying to locate the 'off' switch. The unit was so old and weathered that all the original writing had peeled off and, as I had suspected, the rubber switch covers flapped ineffectively around the base of the switches. The silly thing about an electric fence is that it doesn't really hurt. It's not as bad as hitting your thumb with a hammer or as lasting as a bee sting, you just know it's going to be a very nasty sensation. I hunted around for a good stout dry stick and, holding that in a hanky just to be sure, I pushed off all the switches until the ticking stopped.

Luckily the lambs inside the fenceline had moved away and were too occupied with the business of grazing to notice me as I took down a couple of yards of the temporary wire next to the hedge. Back up on Husham again we circled away and came up behind the strays, driving them along the fence until they came to the gap and popped through, scampering joyfully away to join their friends. I know I had a self-satisfied smile on my face as I replaced the fence and, at the touch of a stick, set the whole thing ticking away again. A very smooth operation, I thought, and it was nice to feel that I had saved Mac a journey just for a couple of escaped lambs.

We took a different route back to Mac's house, Husham flying over the sheep-grazed turf with his wonderful floating paces. We trotted through the hazel woods, pheasants running low away from us, and down the narrow winding tracks through the pine trees, where the sun fell through the branches into pools of sunlight and the smell of fox lay heavy among the bracken. Up and out on to the open downland and away again, while hares scudded away to cover and the cattle stopped mid-chew to watch us pass. Mac's dogs heard us coming half a mile away and barked a warning to their master, who was waiting by his garden gate by the time we reached his cottage.

'All well?' Mac pulled a bar of tobacco and a knife from his pocket and began to pack his pipe.

'Fine.' I slipped off Husham and gave him a pat. 'There were a couple of lambs out in North End, but together we managed to put them back.'

Mac shot me a questioning look.

'It's alright,' I went on. 'I put the fence up properly again and it's all switched on.' I was still feeling rather smug about the way it had all gone so smoothly and was a bit annoyed at his lack of response.

'They're all happy,' I insisted.

Mac put a match to his pipe and drew on it deeply. 'Aye,' he nodded solemnly. 'Aye, they would be happy. They're all supposed to be in North End.'

Chapter Seven

I was milking Bluebell early one morning, sitting uncomfortably on my heels and trying to close my ears to the
excited shrieks coming from Sadsac, who knew that breakfast
was being prepared, when John's figure filled the doorway.
Over the past few days I had often noticed him looking at the
back half of Bluebell's shed with an ominously thoughtful
expression on his face. During the winter we had stored straw
and chicken feed there behind a partition but now, in late
summer, it was almost empty, and I had a feeling that newly
conceived plans were being brooded upon and would shortly
be hatched. I didn't have long to wait.

'Rabbits!' exclaimed John.

I jumped. 'Where?'

'There, in the back of the shed.'

I screwed my head around as far as it would go. 'I can't see
them.'

'No, not now,' he gestured impatiently. 'That's what we
should have. Do you know that one female can produce an
incredible amount of meat in a year? Wire-floored cages,
that's the answer.'

And whipping a steel tape from his pocket he clambered
over an indignant Bluebell, myself and the partition, and
started making a few measurements. 'We could get three
good-sized cages across here, one for the buck, one for the
doe and babies and a weaner cage.'

He stood there, scratching his head thoughtfully. 'Come to
think of it,' he went on in a casual way, 'I seem to remember

63

some Californian rabbits being advertised in the *Gazette* this week. I think I'll just ring and see if they are still there. Perhaps we could go over at the weekend and have a look.' And he wandered away in the direction of the telephone.

I finished milking Bluebell, tipped a couple of pints of the warm, frothy milk into Sadsac's mixing bucket and hung it on a nail out of the chickens' reach while I carried the rest into the kitchen. John was replacing the receiver and looked happy.

'They've still got them, two does and a buck. I said we'd go over Saturday evening.'

'Fine. Where are we going to get the cages?'

James and Richard, grabbing a hurried breakfast before the school bus arrived, began to make quietly for the door.

'I'll get the materials today and the boys can make them before Saturday. You've got two whole evenings, James,' he went on, quelling protest at its source. 'They're simple enough. You can't expect to reap the benefits without putting some effort into it.'

James was genuinely astonished. 'Benefits? Goats' milk and roast rabbit?'

'Bus,' called Joanna from the gate, cutting short the conversation as John searched for a reply. 'This evening,' he yelled after them. 'Don't be late back.'

The rabbit people lived about six miles away, in a farm worker's cottage with an enormous overgrown garden and a sort of a paddock on one side. Tethered there was the smallest nanny goat we had ever seen and a billy goat with a very splendid beard and an exceedingly pronounced presence. We skirted him upwind and approached the back gate through a tangle of bicycles, prams, toys and old mangles. A radio blared from the open doorway and John gave a loud knock, followed by his usual yell of 'Anybody home?'

Immediately the opening was completely filled by a smiling grey-haired lady of extremely comfortable proportions who introduced herself as Mrs Adams. 'An' you must be the lady and gen'leman to see the rabbits,' she beamed, wiping soapy hands carefully on her apron before untying it and hurling it into the darkness of the hallway behind her. 'We keep them in the barn, mind the stinging nettles,' and Mrs Adams paddled off in her slippers along the overgrown path leaving an ample wake for us to slip through unscathed.

Like Murphy's hammer, which was good as new after only three new heads and four new handles, very little of the original barn remained. The structure leaned drunkenly over to one side, propped up with struts at strategic points and patched with corrugated iron and wooden planks. Inside it was dark and the walls and ceiling were festooned with every conceivable treasure collected over the last fifty years or more. Bicycle wheels and bits of leather harness, flowerpots, ladders, broken rakes and pitchforks, enamel jugs, buckets, skeins of binder twine and wooden boxes, bulging sacks and bales of straw. Legless chairs and chairless legs, lanterns, inner tubes and half a car. Everything was snug under half an inch of dust, and everything seemed to be there but rabbits.

'This is Stanley,' said Mrs Adams, stopping by a large crate under a bench. 'He's a bit shy, but I can usually catch him.'

She lowered herself carefully to her knees and opened the door. 'Come on Stanley, come and see these nice people. Come on my sweetheart.' She poked her head inside and the coaxing continued in a muffled voice. Suddenly she lunged forward, head and shoulders disappearing completely into the crate and leaving a large expanse of bottom scarcely covered by the thin cotton skirt and revealing a generous amount of stocking top.

Horrified, John grabbed my arm. 'She'll never get out,' he muttered, looking around for something to use as a lever. Stanley hadn't a hope of making a break for it. Every contour of the opening was blocked, and he must have just given himself up because the crate began to rock violently from side to side as Mrs Adams slipped into reverse. I saw John's hands clenching and unclenching helplessly. His natural desire to do the gentlemanly thing and assist a lady fought desperately with the warning voice that reasonably pointed out that there was nothing for a gentleman to grab. In the end he grabbed the crate, and Mrs Adams came scrabbling backwards, triumphantly hugging a large white rabbit to her breast. Stanley poked a grey splodged nose out from the enveloping folds and turned an enquiring ear in our direction. He was very handsome.

'He's ever so tame really,' panted Mrs Adams. 'Whenever I move him in with a doe I always stop and give him a cuddle and a chat.'

The does were smaller, with the same characteristic markings, and John chose two which he assured me were of good meat-producing conformation. They were popped into cardboard boxes and the lids tied down with binder twine, but Stanley – bless his little cottontail – sat on my lap and had a cuddle and a chat all the way home.

The boys had made a really first-class job of the rabbit cages. They were large and roomy with a neat little wire hayrack in one corner and tins for food and water clipped on to the wire sides. The cage floors were also made of a strong square mesh wire which supported the rabbits' weight without sagging and allowed waste food and droppings to fall onto the straw-covered floor beneath and so kept the cages clean. John fitted them onto a waist-high rail and the shed door was left wide open to the fresh air and sunlight. I couldn't help feeling they would be much happier in their new home than in those boxes beneath the bench in Mrs Adams's barn.

John already had ideas for the floor of the shed beneath the rabbits. About the same time as John had had his rabbit idea, Bert's wife Maggie had asked me to get some shopping for her. I'd called in at their cottage with the parcels on my way back from town and had rounded the corner of her house to come face to face with the most enormous chicken I had ever seen. It was white with sturdy yellow legs, a strong curved beak and wicked eyes. After regarding me beadily for a few seconds it had lumbered off through the rhubarb, brushing the great leaves aside as it passed.

'Her's a Ross, m'dear,' nodded Maggie absent-mindedly taking a knife from her apron pocket and cutting about five pounds of rhubarb, which she laid in my arms without comment. 'We had about twenty of 'em for table birds, but she got sort of left, and then she laid an egg or two so we've let her go on like.' She opened the door of the little greenhouse and plucked half a dozen ripe tomatoes the size of apples and popped them on top of the rhubarb. 'There's a chap in Barfield breeds 'em. They grows ever so fast, and a good one'll give you an eight pound bird on the table in a few months.'

Back home I had told John of my find, and the information had been stored briefly before falling naturally into place.

'We'll put some under the rabbit cages,' he decided. 'They can clear up the food the rabbits waste. If we make a small pen outside the door they could go in and out as they liked, but they wouldn't be able to run around enough to lose weight.'

A couple of phone calls later our next little enterprise was on the way. They arrived in a large crate about a week after the rabbits had settled in. Stocky, well-grown young birds on thick yellow legs which, like the size of a puppy's paws, gave an indication of the dimensions they were likely to reach. We tipped them out on the floor of the rabbits' section, where they immediately started to peck over the straw, finding a wealth of scraps beneath the cages as the rabbits tended to be fairly messy feeders.

Stanley and his wives had settled in well and looked a picture of health, the last cage was finished and in place, and we had hopes that one of the does was already pregnant. Bluebell was fascinated by them and had to be kept out of their half of the shed, as she much preferred their hay to her own and would rob them shamelessly. She had also learned to get the lid off the bin where we kept their food, and she and the kids had flattened half a bag before they were caught.

Sadsac was growing at an unbelievable rate. He had moved into section two of the garden, leaving a well-ploughed section one behind, where the chickens spent many happy hours squabbling over earthworms and leatherjackets. At weekends a number of people would regularly stroll past, lean over the fence and smile at 'The Good Life' as they called it. They came in to buy eggs, then stayed to see the rabbits, play with Bluebell and the kids and scratch Sadsac's back.

' 'E'll make luverly bacon,' commented old Mr Boyes from down in the village, as he gave Sadsac an experimental prod or two. 'You wants to take 'im right off that milk for the last two weeks afore 'e goes, and then 'e won't be too fat.' He inclined a panama'd head towards the back of the house. 'You know what's really good wid a bit o' bacon? Pickled nasturtium seeds,' he went on, not waiting for an answer. His eyes half closed at the thought. 'Oo, they'm luverly wid fried apple rings and a bit o' home cured bacon and fresh eggs. A real good meal that is.' He looked at me sideways. 'My

Missus used to do 'em, they'm ever so easy, just like picklin' onions.' Then, confident that my enthusiasm had been raised, 'C'mon, I'll show 'ee the ones that do best.'

It was important, apparently, to choose the ones that were ripe but not falling to the touch. ('They be a bit 'ard like, better t'ave 'em a bit greener.') I'd never really noticed nasturtium seeds. They just flowered, seeded, reflowered and spread, giving a trouble-free riot of colour behind the house. Now I could see why they were so prolific, seeds were forming by the bushel. I couldn't resist the old man's appeal, so determined to produce some for him 'just like the Missus used to make'. Several days later I presented a delighted Mr Boyes with four closely packed jars of pickled nasturtium seeds and pushed one to the back of the larder for us to try some day.

69

Bert called in on his way to the village one morning, and grinned in amazement at our little farmyard collection.

'Now that's what I calls real intensive farmin',' he chuckled, carefully closing the gate behind him and giving Bluebell a gentle shove as she hopefully probed his jacket pocket. 'So what have you got now, then?'

John counted them off on his fingers. 'Milk, eggs, cheese and yoghurt at the moment, and soon we'll be having poultry, rabbit, pork and bacon.'

'All in that little shed?'

'Shed and garden, yes.'

'My, my,' murmured Bert in wonder, 'who needs a big estate? You must live as well as 'is Lordship.'

'Better,' agreed John, with conviction.

Of course, his Lordship didn't have to go out in his dressing gown to milk the goat for his morning cup of tea. Neither did he have to crawl through the brambles for his breakfast egg or carry buckets of food to his bacon, but in an odd sort of a way I felt that we were still the more privileged.

'An' did you get them from 'is Lordship?' He inclined his head towards the Marans, who were now very handsome in their full plumage, and as a judgement on me had all turned out to be cockerels.

'We hatched them,' I put in quickly, not wanting to involve Maisie in any village gossip, 'from eggs.'

'Aye,' agreed Bert drily, 'that's the usual way. So what's next then? Cider, I suppose, or elderberry wine? Livens winter up no end do a good brew o' wine. Which reminds me why I did come.' He fished around in his pockets and came out with an envelope marked briefly 'Stud'. 'Estate office asked me to drop it by, invitation to a knees-up, I hear.' He peered over John's shoulder expectantly.

John flipped open the envelope and carefully withdrew a gilt-edged card. 'Good Heavens!' His face registered astonishment. 'His Lordship's giving a party.'

'For everyone?'

'You'm jokin' Missus.' Bert gave me a good-humoured nudge. 'Nearest I shall be is car park attendant. No,' he went on, 'heads of staff'll be the lowest invited, if you'll beg pardon for sayin' so.'

'What's it in aid of?'

'Doesn't say, but it's fancy dress – would you believe that? Eastern costume, it says.'

'You can be one o' them dancin' girls, Missus,' grinned Bert wickedly. 'You know, one o' them as wears a brooch in 'er . . .' His voice tailed off as John looked at him sternly. 'Or a sari,' he went on, less enthusiastically, 'they can look quite nice.'

'Well, we've got a month to decide.' My husband put the invitation back in its envelope and handed it to me. 'Right now I must be getting back to the stables. Answer that would you love,' as the telephone started ringing, 'I'll be in the office if someone wants me.'

It was Mac, trying to make himself heard above a background noise of blaring cattle and barking dogs. 'Ha'ye got your runnin' shoes on, Missus?' he asked seriously, breaking off to bellow at the dogs to be quiet. 'Or mebbe you're busy?'

I smiled to myself. This sounded as if it could be much more fun than washing up.

'Not too busy. What are you up to, Mac?'

'His Lordship wants the young bullocks moved from the dairy yards to Home Farm. I'm here wi' ma dogs, but I could do with someone to stop traffic and stand in gaps, if ye have a mind to.'

'Oh, I'd love to. I can be there in ten minutes, is that alright?'

'Aye,' said Mac, and I could almost hear him grinning at my enthusiasm. 'That'll do fine.'

When I reached the yard the cattle had already been brought in from the fields and were excitedly milling around

71

the holding pens. Steam hung in a cloud above them as they pushed and chivvied each other, snorting and coughing wheezily. They had to be walked just over two miles along the narrow, twisty lanes, and Mac had worked out a plan of action. He would go in front, doing his best to keep them down to a walk, and would stop any oncoming traffic. I was to follow with his old sheepdog, keeping the animals together and stopping traffic trying to overtake from behind. When we got near the end of the lane I was to leave the dog to bring up the rear, take a short cut through the fields behind a little copse, and be waiting to direct traffic by the time Mac got to the crossroads. Once on the road to Home Farm I would drop behind again. It was perfect in its simplicity, and Mac handed me a stout, knarled staff. 'Don't ye let *anyone* pass ye,' he warned, tapping the stick significantly.

Mac stood no nonsense from inconsiderate drivers. Woe betide anyone who didn't slow down, or dared to show any form of impatience! Just recently Mac and his dogs had been moving a flock of several hundred sheep along the lanes when, at a tricky crossroads, two ewes had escaped from the mob and made off down the wrong lane. Helpless, Mac had watched them vanish out of sight around the bend, at the same time fighting to keep the rest of the flock together. While deciding whether to risk sending one of the dogs, a car appeared from the direction of the renegade sheep. Thankfully Mac had waved him down. The driver, a smartly dressed middle-aged man, wound down the window.

'Did ye see the sheep?' Mac had enquired eagerly.

The man nodded briefly. 'I did.'

'And?'

The man looked puzzled. 'Well,' he pointed back down the road, 'they were going that way.'

Mac's face had darkened and, twirling like a dervish, he brought his stick smartly down on the car roof above the man's head. 'An ye didna stop 'em?' he screamed incredulously. 'Ye didna stop 'em?'

Understandably indignant, the man had leapt out of his car to inspect the roof, which luckily was undamaged.

'An' do ye know what he said to me?' Mac related to me later, his expression one of hurt pride mixed with incredulity. ' "If ye can't control 'em," he said, "ye shouldn't be allowed loose wi' 'em," he said!'

I gripped the staff firmly. No one would pass me. If they did I knew I would have Mac to deal with.

The bullocks were about ten months old, Friesian–Hereford cross, well grown and heavy. As the gate swung open they crowded eagerly through, fighting for first place and splashing mud and water liberally in all directions. Once out in the yard they gradually settled, and at Mac's call the self-appointed leaders took the mob in a fairly orderly fashion out into the lane. Mac had his work cut out to keep them from running him over, while the dog and I had little to do but trot along quietly, keeping up with them. As we were nearing the little detour I had to make I suddenly realised that there was a car behind me. Big, sleek and shining, it had purred up without notice, and as I turned the well-to-do-looking young man behind the wheel gave me a dazzling smile. I slowed my pace and as the electrically operated window glided silently down, the owner of the smile inclined a well-groomed head towards the bunch of cattle.

'Which way will you take at the crossroads?' he asked pleasantly.

'We're going straight over,' I smiled back.

'Oh, that's fine. I turn left, so I'll just follow on quietly, if I may.'

How nice, I thought, as I jogged back to my place behind the dung-plastered backsides and swishing tails of the jostling bullocks, how considerate and understanding.

On my left I could see the gateway of the little field near the crossroads, and, telling old Shadow to stay back, I hopped over and started my run along the path which followed the back of the copse. The ground climbed steadily and I was about half way along when I suddenly saw the startled form of a deer in front of me. Sheltered from view on all sides, it had been happily tucking into his Lordship's wheat, and as I puffed into sight it took off at top speed into the undergrowth, making a surprising amount of noise for a deer. Usually they just seemed to melt away, but this one had had a real fright and its crashing sent up several cock pheasants who, in turn, let out their echoing alarm calls as they clumsily gained height through the trees. The blood pounded in my ears, and I was panting hard by the time I got to the gate leading back on to the road. I was relieved to see that Mac hadn't yet come into sight. The grass was soaking wet, but I found a fairly dry log and sat down to catch my breath.

It was strange, I thought, that I couldn't hear any noises from Mac or the steers and I began to feel a bit uneasy. The road sloped gently up towards the little wood and I started to wander hesitantly back in that direction. Still they didn't come, and suddenly I found myself running again. Round the corner, by the wood, stood Mac. For once he was speechless, and staring in horror at the car. The beautiful new shining limousine was spattered with mud and scratch marks. Hoof prints were clearly visible on the bonnet and across the roof. The wing mirrors had disappeared without trace, and the aerial stuck crazily out to one side. Tracks of fifty bullocks led up to the car, around both sides of it, over it, and away out of sight. There was no sound from the car.

'Oh, my,' Mac was whispering to himself. 'Oh, my. Oh, my.'

I touched him on the shoulder and he leapt round. 'Is he all right?' In my mind I could see that dazzling smile, and hear the quiet, cultured voice.

'Ah dinna know,' whispered Mac. 'Ah canna look.'

Together we tiptoed up to the window and peered in. On the floor beneath the steering wheel a figure sat with its arms clasped tightly above its head, rocking silently to and fro. Mac tapped on the window and a pale, wild-eyed face peered out

74

from under an armpit. Gone was the well-groomed hairstyle, the suave smile, the immaculate suit. Mac pulled open the door and knelt on the wet verge.

'Are ye all right?'

Wide eyes blinked at him unbelievingly, and a croaking whisper came from the dry lips. 'Bloody 'ell!'

He moved around uncomfortably, looking for a way out of the position he had so easily shot into. He was curled in the foetal position, between the steering wheel and the foot controls, with the hand brake hard up by his right ear. Finally he slithered feet first out of the door and onto the grass, where Mac and I anxiously helped him to his feet. He stood looking numbly at first one of us and then the other.

'Bloody 'ell, I thought I was a goner.' He shook his head in disbelief and his voice quivered. 'One of 'em came over the roof! Over the bonnet and over the roof, I thought he was coming in!' He looked at his wrecked car and gave a quiet sob. 'My boss'll kill me. Are you insured against this sort of thing? 'Cause if you're not . . .'

He was interrupted by the sound of a Land Rover approaching at top speed and round the corner came Jim, the dairyman, his expression a mixture of anxiety, relief and amazement as he took in the little scene before him. Next to him, in the passenger seat, sat a wildly excited Shadow, who leapt out and hurled herself at Mac as the Land Rover slid to a stop. Jim stared at the car, the dented bonnet, and the hoof prints on the roof. He bent down, digging in the mud with his fingers, and came up with a crooked wing mirror minus its mirror. Helplessly he handed it to the owner. 'Bloody 'ell,' he whispered, and we all nodded silently.

He opened the passenger door of the Land Rover and gave the seat a quick brush with his sleeve. 'Hop in, sir. I'll take you to his Lordship's office, we've a bit of sortin' out to do.' He turned to Mac. 'Can you both walk on back to the farm? I've penned the bullocks, I think we'd best leave them where they are at the moment.'

We watched them drive away.

'What happened, Mac?' I still felt as if it was all a bad dream, it had happened so incredibly quickly. Mac leaned heavily on his stick, dug in a pocket for his comforting pipe and packed tobacco carefully into the bowl.

'Weel,' he puffed at it slowly, 'they were comin' along nicely, a bit skittish y'know, but all right, until we came down past the wood. Then these pheasants jest came burstin' oot makin' a hell of a racket, an' the whole lot jest turned aroond an' bolted.' He glanced at me sombrely. ' 'Tis a good job ye had taken the short cut, Missus, ye wouldna be here noo.' He reached down and pulled gently at old Shadow's ears. 'Ah was worried about this ol' lass, likely she would ha' stood her groond y'see, but she must ha' sumhoo dodged 'em.' He drew hard on the pipe until a steady glow appeared. 'Did ye happen to notice that heap of paperwork on the front seat there?' He inclined his head towards the car.

'No, what is it?' I wandered over and peered in. 'Insurance? Looks like he works for an insurance company. Yes, there it is, New World Insurance Co.'

Mac smiled. 'Aye, an' do ye know who deals wi' his Lordship's insurance?'

I shook my head.

Mac grinned and took a long pull at his pipe. 'New World Insurance Co.,' he whispered.

Chapter Eight

NEWS of his Lordship's party had set the whole village buzzing. Most families were involved in some way, if not as guests. The womenfolk were invited to act as waitresses and those who wished were allowed to help behind the scenes in the bars and kitchens. Wild rumours began to spread through the Estate. His Lordship was getting engaged. There was going to be a team of belly-dancers staying at the village pub. Live tigers were going to patrol the grounds, and members of the Royal Family were to fly in by helicopter. One rumour, that sacred white cattle were to mingle with the tigers, was half confirmed by Jim at the dairy. His Lordship had requested that four beef animals of the lightest colour possible be halter trained and docile by the date of the party. The dairyman came to see us, running an anxious hand through his thinning hair, a worried frown on his usually placid face.

'Hell, I'm gettin' a bit long in the tooth for rodeos,' he confided over a cup of strong coffee. 'They'm all wild buggers – never felt a rope on 'em and I, for one, never expected 'em to. Do you think they'd tame same as a horse?'

John heaped sugar into his cup and stirred slowly. 'I really can't say, Jim, but I don't see why not. I'll certainly give you a hand if you want.'

Jim's face brightened a little. 'I'd be that grateful. I'm sure it can be done, but I can't manage on my own, and I didn't get no volunteers from the farm.'

'Well, you pick out the four you want and pen them away

from the rest and then I'll come over and we'll work out a plan.'

It was a couple of evenings later when the phone rang. 'I've picked out four,' Jim informed us. 'Hell, they'm strong, mind, and wild! Bent the gate tryin' to climb over after I'd got 'em penned. I had to put some bars over the top, one of 'em can jump like a cat.'

'Wonderful,' commented John. 'Meet you there tomorrow about ten?'

'Fine,' agreed Jim, 'see you, then.'

The young bullocks had been imprisoned in a large box behind the dairy buildings and greeted us next morning with much suspicious huffing, snorting and tossing of heads. John stood looking at them quietly. 'Well, Jim,' he said at last, 'I know it's cutting it a bit fine, but what I would do is split them up. Keep them separate and a bit hungry so that they start looking forward to seeing you come with a bucket, instead of ganging up against you as soon as you set foot in the door. I reckon, after a few days, if you talk to them quietly, they'll come around. Cattle are naturally curious, aren't they, they'll soon have their heads in the bucket before you can get to the manger.'

Jim looked doubtful. 'Well, I do 'ope you're right. It only gives us just over a week to get them on a halter.'

John was right. A week later a much happier Jim telephoned, a note of triumph in his voice. 'They're much friendlier,' he reported, 'I've been scratchin' the tops of their heads when they're feedin' and they don't move. I reckon we could try the halters now. Can you make it tomorrow morning?'

He met us at the yard gate with a bucket in one hand and a jubilant expression. 'Got the halter on one,' he greeted us. 'Slipped it over when I was scratchin' his head.' He put down the bucket and wiped his hands on the seat of his trousers. 'What I was thinkin',' he went on, 'was if Judy there was to walk ahead with the bucket, he'd follow that. Then if I lead

him perhaps you could have a rope on the other side and be anchor man if we need one.'

'Sounds a good plan,' agreed John.

Actually, with the memory of that flattened car still vivid in my mind, I wasn't at all sure I wanted to be anything but a spectator. Jim handed me the bucket without asking my opinion, however, and together he and my husband headed for the box while I followed fairly reluctantly. The big cream coloured beast looked around from its hayrack as Jim slid back the bolt, and walked forward expectantly looking for the bucket. It seemed remarkably quiet. The dairyman quickly clipped a second rope to the halter and as John pushed open the door Jim handed it to him, and the bullock walked through into the passageway leading to the yard. It seemed puzzled, sniffing each of them in turn and then ambling on until it came to the door into the yard. There it stopped. I had backed into the middle of the yard, watching, as the two men encouraged it with firm pressure on the ropes to move forwards, to no avail.

'Rattle the bucket,' called John.

The effect was dramatic. Instantly the ears shot forward, pinpointing the sound, and then with an enormous bound the great beast leapt out of the doorway, and straight towards me, dragging Jim and John along like corks on a string. The yard was surrounded by a three-foot wall, topped with two rails. It had been designed to hold cattle, but it was no barrier to me. The thing that really astonished me was not the way I cleared the wall and ducked under the rail in one graceful, fluid movement, but the fact that I was still clutching the bucket when I landed on the other side. And as my feet hit the floor, Jim's words came singing back to me: 'One of 'em can jump like a cat.' The bullock, cheated of its breakfast, was bucking determinedly while both men hung on, desperately trying to dig their heels into solid concrete.

'Bring the bucket back,' yelled John, doing a nifty bit of footwork on the corner.

Bring it back? He was joking! My husband cantered past on lap two, he didn't look in a jocular mood. 'The bucket,' he howled, through clenched teeth, 'chuck in the bucket.'

I dropped the bucket over the wall, where it landed with a crash that was music to the bullock's ears. Breakfast! It did a swift right-angled turn. Jim was on the inside, and with an incredible ballet leap, seemingly unhampered by wellies, he managed to avoid the charge and hang on to the rope. John, however, was on the outside and had no chance to check his momentum as the rope slipped through his fingers. His legs kept going in a desperate attempt to stay ahead of his body and succeeded in keeping him more or less upright until the wall stopped them and his body overtook them again. He lay, gasping quietly, across the top of the little barrier, while just the other side of the rails from me Jim was still holding his piece of rope as the bullock unconcernedly licked up the spilled grain and pushed the bucket around with his nose to get the last bits.

Breakfast over at last, he wandered quietly away in the direction of his box, leading a rather confused-looking Jim. My husband followed them wearily. I couldn't help feeling that I had spoilt the overall plan of things, and so when the three of them reappeared in the doorway I decided that probably the most helpful thing I could do was to stay quiet. The bullock was much calmer on his second time round the yard, and after ten minutes' steady walking he was put back inside and sacred cow number two was duly haltered. This time they dispensed with the bucket idea and just hung on grimly until the bucks subsided, following this up with another ten minute walk, at a fairly brisk pace.

'I reckon that'll do for one day,' decided Jim, as he slammed the door shut on the second bullock and put a hand to his aching back. 'If you're still game to give me a hand perhaps we could try the other two tomorrow.'

My assistance was no longer sought, and John and Jim carried out the rest of the training on their own, until three days before the party, when I was casually invited to go along and see the results.

Frank Woods, a quiet, solidly built tractor driver who sometimes gave a hand with the cattle, was standing in the yard with Jim when we arrived. As the car pulled into the driveway the dairyman hurried into the buildings and came back, leading one of the bullocks, which he handed to Frank. John followed him back inside again and they both came back with an animal each. 'Here we are,' grinned Jim, 'this'n's yours,' and he carelessly threw me the end of the rope as he scuttled away for number four.

'Quiet as a lamb,' my husband assured me, then went on, 'we thought we'd take them through his Lordship's gardens so that they can see the tents and things.'

The grounds of the Manor had been trimmed and tidied.

Marquees had arrived and swelled overnight into dining halls, bars and dancing areas. Coloured lights were strung through the trees and floodlights were trained upon the Manor House itself. With a sacred cow each we wandered slowly along the garden paths and grassy avenues between the ancient great trees, skirting the tents and bandstand where peafowl screamed and strutted. Workmen were still busy building platforms and stringing up lights and, as we crossed the main drive to circle back towards the dairy, his Lordship's Estate manager came hurrying up, waving a clip board.

'That's where they are going to be,' he informed us briefly, 'in the middle of the lawn there.' He pointed in passing. 'Tethered there,' he called back, and was gone.

John and Jim exchanged glances. Tethered. No one had said anything about them being tethered. 'Back to the drawing board,' sighed John. Forty-eight hours to go. At the dairy we tethered them securely, two on each side of a rail, with a heap of hay to keep them happy, crossed our fingers and left them in Jim's tender care.

Our costumes had arrived. John had chosen gaily striped Arab robes with a flowing head-dress secured by a circle of black woollen rope. The outfit came complete with an extremely genuine-looking beard and moustache, and the overall effect was distinctly evil.

'Psst. Got any picture post cards?' grinned Bert when he was invited in to see.

Mine was that of a very demure dancing girl, with filmy baggy pants, silken top and a matching jewelled cap. The nearest I came to wearing a brooch in my navel was a jewelled belt below a bare midriff, and the lower part of my face was covered with a veil.

'Wow!' approved Bert, earnestly. 'Wow!'

The great day arrived at last, and as evening approached we went with Jim to tether the sacred cattle in their allotted place. Everywhere people rushed hither and thither, carrying trays and boxes, musical instruments, flowers and microphones. Men on ladders made last-minute adjustments and the caterers counted the plates and stacked them in great piles at the end of the buffet tables.

'Four bulls in a china shop,' observed John uneasily, and made a wide detour. The cattle securely anchored and pacified with more sweet hay than they could possibly eat, we hurried home to bath and change.

It was dusk when we left the house. Bluebell stared at us in utter amazement, then took off down the garden with a snort of alarm to hide behind the chicken house until we had

driven out of sight. For the first time since our arrival we entered the Manor grounds by the front gate. A field on the right of the entrance had been turned into a temporary car park, attended by a handful of his Lordship's farm and Estate staff, looking slightly uncomfortable in stiffly laundered white coats issued for the occasion. We were waved into position alongside the Mercedes and the Bentleys by Bert, who had been watching out for the little Renault. 'Enjoy yerselves,' he opened the door for me, and gave a mock bow. 'Bring us back a packet o' crisps.'

The Manor grounds had been turned into a fairyland of lights and fountains, and echoed with music and laughter. Already the entertainments were well under way. A tightrope walker seemed to be floating on air as she danced along an invisible wire, while a spotlight picked out plump belly-dancers undulating across the lawn. Further on a fire eater breathed long tongues of flame into the night sky, watched by a group of his Lordship's guests in colourful costume. Maisie came past in a black dress and white apron carrying a tray of brimming wine glasses. 'Red or white, Madam?'

'Oh, thanks Maisie, white please.'

'And white for me too, please Maisie,' added John.

Maisie frowned and peered closely from one to the other. 'Well,' she said at last, 'I dunno, you got me foxed, 'oo are you?'

We kept her guessing for a while, but as I had to remove my yashmak to drink we finally gave in.

'I like this,' said John, trying to keep his moustache out of the wine. 'If nobody recognises us it's as good as being invisible. Come on, let's mingle a bit.'

The costumes were varied and extravagant. Mandarins rubbed shoulders with Arabs, sari'd women chatted to skimpily clad dancing girls. Candle-shaped lights adorned the rose gardens and his Lordship's Estate manager in a long shirt-like gown and a fez trotted busily along the line of lights adjusting one here and there.

John nudged me. 'Look,' he whispered, 'Wee Willy Winkie.'

We passed the sacred cattle, munching hay steadily, with eyes half closed, and spent ten minutes watching a determined snake charmer wooing what may or may not have been an empty basket. At the edge of the lawn a group of people were staring upwards into the branches of an oak tree. As we joined them a little chap in a loin cloth and a lot of burnt cork grinned at us as he left. 'They say you should never look up at a seagull,' he commented. 'I should think that would apply even more to a peacock,' and we realised a roosting bird was the object of interest.

John grabbed my arm. 'Good Lord, look at that!' He pointed ahead to a man in a turban lounging comfortably on a bench beneath one of the great cedar trees. At his feet, watching the people go by, lay a full-grown tiger. 'I wonder if the sacred cows have see it!' I was relieved to see that it was on a chain, but nevertheless we gave it a wide berth.

People were beginning to drift towards the buffet tables and we joined the cosmopolitan flow. Great branching candelabra spread a flickering light over the sumptuously decorated dishes. Joints of beef, pink and succulent, plates of chicken drumsticks with little frills around the ankles, bowls of green salads. There were fresh whole salmon, and kebabs on long skewers lying on beds of rice and peppers. Dishes of taramasalata, piles of warm pitta bread and every type of fruit one could wish for. Maisie and her team kept the wine glasses filled while his Lordship's guests did justice to his hospitality. We had only glimpsed our host momentarily in the candlelight, his jewelled turban and superb robes setting him apart even in that magnificent setting. As we ate, eastern music played and the belly-dancers gyrated bravely among the tables. A few of the less well-equipped but fairly agile guests joined in, and before long there was a knees-up in full swing that would have delighted Bert if he could have been there. The evening passed quickly in a haze of wine, a disarrangement of music, and a surfeit of good food. Perhaps, after all, we didn't live quite as well as his Lordship.

At last we rose and made our way towards his table, to give our thanks and take our leave. He accepted our gratitude with a brief nod, and without, I am sure, the least idea of who we were. As we were leaving the marquee John suddenly paused, frowned a little and then walked determinedly back to the buffet table where there lay the mutilated remains of the feast. Amazed that he could still be hungry I followed out of curiosity. 'Excuse me.' My husband caught the eye of one of the hovering waiters. He looked up and down the table, realising the futility of his next question, but it had to be asked. 'Do you, by any chance, happen to have a packet of crisps?' Then, seeing the waiter's faint look of surprise, he added quickly, 'To take home, for a friend.'

The man smiled and nodded understandingly. 'I think we can find you something, Sir,' he whispered and to my embarrassment he began to heap a selection of the remains into a napkin which he folded carefully and handed to John, who gratefully slipped it beneath his robe. We found Bert pacing up and down, yawning, at the car park gate. John sidled up to him, one hand hidden.

'You want to see picture postcard?' he hissed, then produced the package with a flourish.

'Well, I'm blessed.' Bert unfolded it carefully and his face broke into a wide grin. Slices of cold meat, pitta bread, a chicken leg and a dainty bunch of watercress.

'Sorry about the crisps,' apologised John.

Chapter Nine

JOHN was on the phone when I came into the kitchen, gingerly balancing five newly found eggs in the front of my jumper and trying not to spill the milk.

'No trouble at all,' he was saying, 'only too glad to help.' He replaced the receiver and sat down again at the breakfast table. 'That was Mac,' he explained, reaching for another slice of toast. 'His Lordship has arranged for some people to go and look at the sheep tomorrow and Mac wanted some help.'

I carefully decanted the eggs into a bowl. 'What does he want you to do?'

'Not me, you.' John poured two cups of coffee and pushed one towards me.

'Me? How can I help?'

'Well, he has to stay and show these people around, but he had already sorted out some lambs to go to the market in Westborne. Obviously he can't do both,' he stirred a second spoonful of sugar into his coffee, 'so I said you'd take them.'

'How many?'

'Twenty-five.'

'*Twenty-five*? In the *Renault*?'

'No, not the Renault,' sighed my husband patiently. 'You'll take the Land Rover and trailer.'

'But I've never driven the Land Rover and trailer!' I was horrified. 'I don't even know where the market is in Westborne. Come to that, I don't even know Westborne.'

'It's childishly simple,' stated my husband, airily, obliquely implying that it would be no problem to anyone but a woman. 'Anyway, Mac will have them all ready for you by seven tomorrow morning.'

'John,' I tried again, 'that trailer is enormous. I've never even towed it before, let alone through a strange town. What happens if I have to back up? I wouldn't have a hope, I never could get the hang of it – you must remember me trying with that little camping trailer we had. I'm about the only woman in the world to have jack-knifed a mini.'

'Why are you going to need to back up?'

'Well, you know these lanes. If I meet a car in a narrow place.'

'Then you smile at him, look helpless, and he'll back up.'

'What happens if it's a woman?'

'She'll probably be only too glad to show she's a better driver than you are,' grinned my husband, infuriatingly. 'Come on,' he added, adopting a confident, fear-banishing tone. 'You know you can do anything you set your mind to. This really isn't difficult, Mac wouldn't have suggested it if he didn't think you could cope.'

Mac's complete confidence in me had ruined my day.

I awakened at five the next morning with an anxious feeling in my stomach but determination in my heart. Childishly simple, eh? Right!

Bluebell was a bit surprised at being milked two hours early, but sensing my mood she wisely decided not to argue. It was 6.30 as I climbed the hill to Mac's cottage. The sun was already warm, and the air clear and fresh. The dogs heard me coming, and sent up a barking that was echoed by others in the village below, until a single bellow from Mac quietened the collies and restored peace to the valley. A cockerel with feathers on its legs crowed a challenge and went scurrying back into the overgrown garden to join the assortment of chicken, ducks and geese that scratched or preened beside the little, feather-littered pond. Mac, in shirtsleeves, old navy trousers and waistcoat, raised his crook in greeting, sent his dogs back inside, and carefully closed the gate.

'Good of ye t'help oot,' he greeted me warmly. 'Ah knew ye woodna let me doon.'

I remembered with shame my immediate reaction to his call for help. 'Mac, I've never driven this outfit before.' I eyed it nervously. The lambs were already on board, peeping out through the side vents and milling about with a restlessness that caused the trailer to shake and groan alarmingly.

'Och,' Mac made a dismissive gesture, 'there's nothin' to it. Jest remember to take the corners a bit wider than usual so that the trailer doesna go onto the pavement.' He opened the driver's door and plumped up the floral-covered cushion on the seat. ''Tis best not to go above forty,' he suggested, 'otherwise the trailer rocks the Land Rover and spoils the steering a wee bit.' He leaned in and checked it was in neutral. 'Ye have eight gears, ye shouldna want more than that,' he added confidently, giving the steering wheel a rub with his sleeve, 'but she does sometimes jump oot of second on hills, best hold it in and keep your foot near the brake jest in case.' He stood aside for me to climb aboard, shut me in firmly and stepped back with a morale-boosting smile. 'Have a good journey.' He glanced at the front wheel as I turned the key and the engine roared into life. 'Spare wheel and jack in the back,' he called helpfully, as we moved forwards, 'but ye shouldna need 'em.'

As we rattled and bumped down the track to the road I had a quick mental picture of myself, hunched grim-faced over the wheel, every muscle taut as I willed the trailer to ride steadily and the gear lever to stay in second. 'Relax,' I told myself, 'you're attracting disaster.'

We negotiated the gateway and crossed the road without mishap, passed two oncoming cars with room to spare and climbed slowly out of the valley without missing any gears. By the time we had reached the main road I had got the feel of the thing, the extra adrenalin had made me light-headed and carefree, and I was beginning to enjoy myself. The main road was wide and there was little traffic as we bowled confidently along the straight and swept round the gentle bends, until suddenly, going down a bit of an incline, I got the feeling I was being pushed. I glanced at the speedometer and found to my surprise that it was registering fifty. Remembering Mac's warning I braked gently and the Land Rover fought gamely to resist the force of the trailer that was trying to overtake it. We lurched dangerously around a bend and up a gentle hill, which fortunately slowed the whole thing down to a manageable speed. 'Overconfidence', I warned myself, 'won't do you any good either.'

By the time we had reached the outskirts of the town the traffic was beginning to build up and we slipped out of our quiet approach road into a stream of shiny cars heading for the town by-pass. Mac had given me directions. Left at the first junction, third exit at the first roundabout, then follow the market signs on the left. Childishly simple! We had only travelled a few hundred yards before traffic came to a standstill in all three of the lanes leading to the roundabout. Leaning out of the window I could see a young policeman walking down our line of cars, stopping and speaking to each driver.

'Been an accident, Miss,' he explained as he got to me. He looked fairly cheerful about it. 'Market road's closed for about half an hour, be best for you to park somewhere and come back.'

I stared at him blankly. As someone who had difficulty in parallel parking the Renault, I could see little hope of my parking something three times as long, using only forward gears. The traffic began to move forward and I followed it aimlessly, racking my brain for some helpful idea. Apart from driving round and round the roundabout for half an hour, nothing sprang to mind. I didn't know where any of the other roads led, but as I drew up to the roundabout I saw to my relief that the first exit was a quiet, shady avenue. I didn't have time to read the sign, strictly speaking I was in the wrong stream of traffic, but it looked my best bet. I flashed the indicators and nosed across, taking advantage of the fact that, besides being bigger than the cars around me, the old Land Rover was less allergic to scratch marks. Suitable evasive action must have been taken by them all, for we turned gratefully into that peaceful, inviting little lane without a horn blown in anger. As we left the noisy, impatient tangle of vehicles behind, I sighed with relief and relaxed once more.

The lane was narrow and edged with beautifully spaced beech trees that met overhead, forming a graceful arch. It was cool and pleasant, and I wondered how the avenue of trees had come to be planted so many years ago, admiring the way they had been maintained. It wasn't until I rounded a bend and came face to face with a pair of gigantic wrought iron gates, hung on great stone pillars with haughty looking eagles on top, that I realised I was in a private driveway. No wonder there hadn't been much traffic. I pulled up and returned the eagles' stony stare. There was simply no place to go except forward. Even if I had wanted to reverse, the closely growing beech trees made it impossible.

Thornley House, stated the sign, Private. Fortunately the gates were open and we crept cautiously through. No one seemed to be around. The driveway curved round to the left and then went out of sight behind great clumps of rhododendron bushes and ornamental trees. I wished fervently that the trailer wouldn't rattle so. Thornley House. I was trying to remember where I had heard the name before. I knew it was something to do with a horse, and as I reached the end of the drive and came suddenly face to face with the huge rambling mansion, it came to me. John had collected a mare from Thornley House, it belonged to Lord Dulton, an old friend of his Lordship. I had met him once, soon after our arrival at the Stud, a pompous, humourless man with expressionless eyes and a tendency towards recurring gout. Not one to take kindly to a dung-spattered Land Rover towing two dozen lambs up his neatly raked driveway between knife-edged lawns. Doubtless his Lordship will hear of this, I thought glumly.

The drive opened out into a wide gravelled area in front of the stone steps leading to the massive front door. Slowing to a tiptoe I put the steering on full lock and in less than a breathless minute we had done an about turn and were heading briskly back down the drive. I scanned the mirror anxiously for signs of detection. They had probably taken my number and were ringing the police right now. Once safely through the gates we were soon back to the roundabout, where the traffic was still in a jam-packed snarl-up. The road to the market was now directly opposite and, peering across, I could see a line of lorries drawing slowly along towards the market entrance. It looked as if things were beginning to get sorted out over there. Before long the last lorry had moved up enough to give me room to join the queue so, checking the traffic on my right, I slammed the Land Rover into gear and headed for the gap. As I moved out across the round-about two cars came out of the road on my left and slotted themselves neatly in behind the last lorry. I pulled up and glared at them furiously. That really wasn't playing fair! I heard a tap on the window. It was the young policeman again, but he didn't look quite so cheerful.

'You can't stay there, Miss,' he stated flatly.

'I didn't want to stay here,' I pointed out with as much patience as I could muster, 'I was going where those two cars are.'

'Well there's no room, Miss. No one can get past you here, you're blocking the whole roundabout. Move on, please.' And with an expression that quelled further discussion he stepped back and waved me firmly out of the next exit, which was clearly signposted 'Town Centre'. I wouldn't stand a chance of either parking or turning if I followed that road to its logical conclusion. A lay-by came into view on my left and I turned into it, switched off the engine and tried to look at things calmly. I got out and checked the lambs. They were quite unconcerned. The road back to the roundabout was still jammed with cars. I got back in and sat looking at them hopelessly.

The driver of a van opposite me waved to attract my attention. 'Do you want to turn round?' he asked in fluent sign language. I nodded. 'Come on then, I'll let you in,' he gestured silently. I hesitated. I wasn't sure that I could do it in one sweep. I could see me stuck right across the road, stopping traffic from every direction. The driver in the car behind the van was grinning. 'Go on,' he joined in the soundless conversation, 'you can do it, easy!' And to give encouragement he backed up a couple of feet and motioned the driver behind him to do the same. The van driver followed suit and a gap of about twelve feet appeared. Now they were all watching, and as the rest of the line moved forwards they made enthusiastic windmill motions with their arms in a combined attempt to propel me forwards. It seemed ungrateful not to try. After all, if I was going to hit anything I was going to hit them. I switched on, engaged first, put her on full lock, let in the clutch slowly and aimed for the gap. We made it with a couple of feet to spare, and I felt a delighted wave of silent cheering go up from the cars behind us.

We crept safely around the roundabout once more, down the market road and finally slowed outside the market gates. On my right lorries were parked along the roadside, also waiting to get in. The young policeman materialised again, but this time he looked apologetic. 'I don't know how to say this, Miss,' he began, 'but those lorries parked over there were here before you. I'd like you to go on up the road, turn around and join in behind them, please.'

He made it sound so simple. Turn around. In front of me an enormous truck with a second three-tier trailer on the back was doing just that. An effortless, faultless, three-point turn. I wondered if he would do the same for me if I asked nicely, but the young policeman was looking a bit impatient again. I moved on to find myself behind another Land Rover and trailer. As we came to a lay-by on our right, he flashed his indicator, swung hard to his right and was round – with me right on his tail. Nothing else could stand in my way, I told myself triumphantly, I was in the right queue, facing the right way, at the right market. Gradually we moved up until, at last, I was driving in through the gates. The young policeman popped his head in at the window. 'Congratulations, Miss,' he grinned, 'I just knew you'd make it!'

Once inside everything was organised. I was waved on until I had reached the entrance to the next lot of vacant pens, then one man let down the ramp and two more chivvied the lambs along and slammed the gates behind them. Behind the market was a huge lorry park, and I cruised along slowly until I found a space that I could drive into and out of without having to make any difficult manoeuvres. Switching off the engine, I slid out of the hot cab. I had earned a cup of coffee and a look around.

Sheep of every known breed, plus a few puzzlers, called loudly on all sides, as I made my leisurely way through the pens. I could get to like sheep, I thought, but I'd prefer to get to know them as individuals rather than numbers in a flock. I passed a pen of Jacobs, with their beautifully marked black and white fleeces and distinctive array of horns. Now that was a good sheep to have. Leaning on the rails I studied them, collecting together my ragged nerves and trying not to think about the journey home. I felt a hand on my shoulder.

'So there ye are, Missus, there ye are. What kept ye?' Mac was standing there, cool as a cucumber, in his smart market day suit and shiny shoes. I stared at him as if he'd just been beamed down from another planet.

'How did you get here?' I whispered in disbelief. 'You're supposed to be showing his Lordship's guests around.'

'Och, they telephoned jest after ye left. Postponed it 'til

next week. So I thought I may as weel cum along an' see the opposition.'

How could he stand there so calmly and say that? He could probably have stopped me before I'd gone through Woodford. I fixed him with a level stare. 'So you could have brought the lambs after all?'

Mac beamed, and patted me on the arm. 'Aye, weel, I could have,' he admitted coyly, 'but I know how it es. Ye like tae help when ye can, an' – weel – ah dinna want t'spoil yer fun.'

Chapter Ten

JOANNA lay flat on the floor in front of the fire, her nose buried deeply in the pages of the *Gazette*. 'Three-year-old mare,' she read out, longingly. 'Well handled, no vices, ready to bring on. Make 14.2 h.h. Oh – £800.' There was silence for a few minutes, then: 'Absolute bargain. 15 h.h. four-year-old gelding. Very fast and strong, not beginner's ride, make good hunter in right hands.'

'Please buy it,' translated John, reading between the lines. 'It's run away with everyone and we can't handle it.'

Joanna sighed. 'I expect they'd want more than a hundred pounds for it anyway.'

For the past year she had saved every penny she could earn towards her dream horse. It was all very well living among all those beautiful, incredibly expensive animals in his Lordship's stables, but she had set her heart on having a young horse of her own. 'I want to teach it everything myself,' she had explained. 'I want a horse with an open mind.'

We both understood how she felt, and knew that she was perfectly capable of achieving her goal. She had, since the age of four, miraculously survived a succession of wicked little ponies, and thanks to them had developed into a strong, determined yet sensitive rider. Every week she scanned the 'Horses for Sale' column in the *Gazette* in the sure belief that, somehow, her hard-earned hundred pounds would be just enough to buy her dream.

'Six hundred ponies,' she suddenly exclaimed, excitedly, 'broken and unbroken, to be sold by auction.'

'New Forest pony sales,' I guessed.

'That's right. I might get something there with the money I've saved.'

'You might,' agreed John, 'but it'll be completely wild, and I doubt if you'll get anything old enough to ride for a while with that amount.'

'So I would have time to get it good and friendly,' pointed out our daughter, practically. 'I don't mind taking a long time about it, as long as I can do it all on my own.'

'It would be fun to go and have a look,' I suggested.

'Well, if we go and look we had better take the horsebox,' put in my husband, matter of factly, 'because with you two together we shall almost certainly come back with something.'

'It's on a Thursday,' grinned Joanna, 'I shall have to be sick.'

The thought of missing school for a day made the whole thing even more appealing. On the Wednesday evening before the sale the excitement was intense. Our daughter arrived home from school with a flushed face and glowing eyes that could easily have been misinterpreted as the beginnings of a fever, and lent more weight to the fact that she intended to be sick. She was well enough, however, to diligently clean out the horsebox and equip it with straw, haynet and a halter, count her money carefully and seal it in a large brown envelope, and bed down one of the big weaning boxes – just in case!

By 6.30 the following misty morning we were on our way, each of us as childishly excited as the other. The headlights of the big lorry cut through the darkness of the autumn morning, reflecting in the roadside puddles and chasing away the still sleepy birds that had come down for a drink and an early morning bath. The cab was warm and cosy and as we climbed steadily out of the valley we suddenly found ourselves in bright sunshine, in a clear sparkling world above the clouds, with a blue sky overhead and swirling white mists

97

below. It was a day for dreams to come true, and Joanna sang happily to herself as we drove, nudging me to join in the choruses, while John tapped out the rhythm on the steering wheel.

The villages were awake and tractors already busy in the fields, while through the towns the streets were quiet before the bustle of the working day. We shared our daughter's excitement completely, for like her we were playing truant! It was ages since we had just taken a day off during the week, and it gave an extra special feeling to the whole affair.

Around us the countryside began to change. The neat patchwork fields were replaced by wide stretches of open moorland, reaching as far as the horizon, knee deep in heather and marshy grasses, speckled with clumps of gorse and here and there a lonely weathered fir tree. We were back in country I knew, and for a moment I was Joanna's age again, remembering the joy and excitement of standing with that rope in my hand, knowing that the shaggy, wild-eyed, suspicious colt at the other end was mine. I remembered the almost tangible freshness about him. In his eyes, beyond the surface nervousness and mistrust, there had been just a hint of that open-mindedness that our daughter sought. From somewhere beyond those eyes there had been a shy, delicate telepathic wave that had offered friendship in return for understanding, hesitant to believe and slow to trust, but it was there. It had taken patience and the willingness to learn on both sides to develop that fragile bond into a strong and confident partnership, the joy of which can only be known by those in whom a horse unreservedly puts his trust. He was a part of my life that I would always remember with warmth, and now here was my daughter eager to find her own way around the mind of a horse. History, it seemed, was coming its full circle.

The sales were held in and around a group of pens out on the open Forest. Ponies were brought from all over the area, some herded in by riders on horseback, some driven into lorries and transported there by road. Others, already broken and up for sale, were brought in trailers or ridden there across country. Cars, lorries, people and ponies were everywhere, and already the yards were fairly full of mares, yearlings, foals and geldings. Some kicked irritably, others stood quietly while men and boys with white rags on long sticks herded still more animals into the bulging pens. Mares called repeatedly for their foals, which had been taken away to be sold under separate lot numbers, men shouted and lorries revved their engines to back down to the narrow yard entrances.

We parked under some trees, bought a catalogue and pushed our way through to the first row of pens. The ponies came in all shapes, sizes and colours, from the old pot-bellied mares with ragged manes and broken hooves to foals with patches of fluffy baby fur still mingling with their young coats. Joanna darted ahead, eagerly scanning each pen.

'Come and look.' She beckoned us to one that had taken her eye. It wasn't attractive, by any stretch of the imagination, but it was big. It also had wall eyes which gave it a wild, startled look. The catalogue didn't mention age.

'Seven,' announced John, peering at its teeth. 'Too old.'

'No, no, four, Sir!' A round little man in a brown hairy tweed jacket, breeches and a cap plucked anxiously at John's sleeve. 'He's four. Good strong horse he is, too.'

John obligingly looked again. 'Seven,' he repeated.

'No, Sir. He's four, as I stand here, Sir.'

'Well,' said my husband patiently, 'I think, Joanna, he's a bit too strong for you to manage entirely on your own.' He glanced at the horse's owner. 'At seven he'd be a bit too big, but at four he's still got some growing to do.'

'Oh, he won't grow any more, Sir.' The little man had dodged round the other side of us now. 'He'll not grow any more, not 'im. And quiet as a lamb, Miss,' he turned to Joanna with a benevolent smile, 'can do anything this horse, jump, gymkhana, very good ride he is. My kids can do

99

anything with 'im. What was it you wanted to do with 'im, my dear?'

'School an untouched horse,' smiled Joanna sweetly. The man opened his mouth and closed it again. There was no answer to that one.

We moved on slowly among the pens, stopping now and again as something attracted Joanna's attention, but it began to look, after nearly an hour's searching, as if everything was either too old, too young or too small.

'Look,' called Joanna, stopping by one of the last pens. 'Can you look this one up in the catalogue?'

It was a very pretty grey pony of around fourteen hands. 'Six years old. Connemara. Broken,' read John. 'She'll be expensive, I'm afraid.'

Joanna was looking miserable.

'Look,' said John, 'why don't we split up for half an hour. There are still a few coming in. Make a note of any numbers that might be right and we'll see how much they fetch when the bidding starts. You never know,' he added comfortingly, 'prices might not be too high, it just depends on who wants them.'

Left on my own I wandered back the way we had come. At every pen I stopped and examined each animal thoroughly and critically. I knew the wrong pony wouldn't be a cheap pony in the end, no matter how low its price, but I shared my daughter's disappointment. I had been right around the yard for a second time when the auctioneer's bell went for the start of the bidding. We had arranged to meet by the sale ring and looking across I saw John making his way in my direction. It was as I turned towards him that I noticed the back end of a pony. I don't know why it should have stopped me, except that it was a very beautifully shaped back end! The tail swept almost to the ground, the legs were long and sturdy, and that part of the middle I could see was slim and young looking. I moved closer and as the others in the pen shifted their positions a well-shaped shoulder came into

view, a shaggy mane and at last a pretty little head with big
shining eyes. She was bay, with a little coronet of white
around one back fetlock, and as the breeze stirred her mane a
small white diamond shape showed through the heavy
forelock. As I stood there I suddenly realised that from the
other side of the pen John had also discovered her, and I saw
him start to thumb through the catalogue.

'Sixteen months old,' he read, as I joined him, 'thirteen
hands, New Forest, eligible for registration.' She just seemed
to stand out from the rest. John went off in search of Joanna
and led her back to the pen. He had no need to point the filly
out, it was love at first sight!

'I don't know how much she'll grow,' warned John. 'She
may make fourteen hands, she's good and long in the legs,
but she won't make any more.'

'She's lovely.' Joanna was leaning on the rails, spellbound.
'Oh, I do hope she's not too expensive.'

The bidding was in full swing as the foals were driven into

the tiny sale ring one by one, sold and driven out again. By the exit gate a band of jolly, red-faced men laughed and joked among themselves, raising a hand casually to register their bids or just nodding their agreement as the price was raised. They seemed to be buying most of the foals, and obviously had money to spare.

'Butchers,' remarked a quiet voice behind me, and I turned to see an elderly woman in a plastic mac and head-scarf, watching the scene with sadness on her face. She nodded towards the laughing group. 'Butchers,' she repeated. 'All those foals are going for meat.'

I hoped Joanna hadn't heard. The foals were making a very good price, it was more than likely that the filly would be more than she could afford, and we were in no position to help her financially. And I couldn't bear the thought of that lovely little filly going to the red-faced men. The last of the foals had been sold and the auctioneer was starting on the yearlings as John turned to Joanna.

'Are you sure about this?' he asked seriously. 'The other two, the wall-eyed horse and the Connemara, they will be sold after the filly. It will be too late to think about them if you get her.'

'No, she's the right one.' Our daughter was emphatic.

The first yearling went for sixty pounds, the next one for sixty-five. The red faces seemed to have plenty of money to spend. I began to feel more hopeful as nothing seemed to be going for more than seventy pounds. Then suddenly she was there; trotting into the ring with a toss of her mane, she stood regarding the crowd carelessly as the bidding began. It started at sixty and rose steadily. Obviously we hadn't been the only ones to spot that special little creature. Red faces were bidding too, and as the price rose to ninety-five I couldn't look at Joanna. At last it reached one hundred, then one hundred and five. There was a lull, then one hundred and ten. The auctioneer's hammer crashed down. 'Name?' called the auctioneer. 'Vowles,' answered John.

Joanna couldn't speak. In true female fashion she was so happy she wanted to cry and so overwhelmed she couldn't really believe it.

'Thank you,' she kept whispering, hanging on to John's arm. 'Thank you.'

We went with her to the auctioneer's little hut where the carefully sealed envelope, plus a bit, was solemnly exchanged for a piece of paper giving her authority to take her pony.

The filly was standing calmly in one of the side pens as Joanna ducked under the rails and approached her quietly. She made no fuss as she slipped the soft white halter on, and we followed the pair out of the yards and down the track to the horsebox. They walked her around as I let down the ramp and spread the straw, then without a moment's hesitation the little pony followed Joanna straight up into the box. She certainly was a very self-assured young animal.

'Can we find out who sold her?' asked Joanna. 'It would help if I knew as much as I could about her.'

'We can ring the auctioneers later,' suggested John, 'they'll be too busy now to look up that sort of thing.'

Joanna made herself a comfortable nest in the compartment next door to the filly. The box was fitted with a bell that rang in the cab, so if she did panic for any reason Joanna could stop us. We trundled home quietly, avoiding any quick braking or sharp turns that might upset our very precious cargo. She travelled well and John was puzzled. 'Either she's done all this several times before, or she's incredibly placid for a youngster,' he remarked to me quietly, as back at the stables our daughter led her proudly down the ramp and into the waiting loosebox. Jane and Debbie were as excited as we were, as we all gathered round the wide doorway to watch the filly investigate her new home. Beautiful, they agreed, absolutely perfect.

'So what are you going to call her?' asked Debbie.

'Well, I was thinking', our daughter pointed to the well-defined white mark on the pony's forehead, 'that looks exactly like a diamond, it should have something to do with that.'

'Well, you don't want anything too ordinary,' put in Jane. 'She must have a very special name. How about Solitaire, that's a diamond.'

'Solitaire,' repeated Joanna slowly, rolling the new name around her tongue. Then she nodded. 'Yes, I like that – but it needs something else.'

'Did you enjoy the sale?' asked Debbie.

I shook my head. 'Not as much as I expected. It's a bit heart-breaking really. As far as I can see most of them are sold for meat.' I nodded towards the filly: 'The butchers were bidding for her too, she was lucky to have come out of it alive.'

Debbie shuddered. 'That would have been criminal. Well, she's lucky Joanna found her.'

Joanna was gazing across the fields, a smile on her lips. 'And now,' she daydreamed quietly, 'we have our next contestant in the ring, Miss Joanna Vowles on Lucky Solitaire.'

We rarely saw our daughter over the next few weeks. She was gone at dawn to 'play games' with Lucky, and back just in time to change for school. Fortunately she had trained the school bus driver long ago. Not only did he wait for her when she wasn't there, I even saw him back up to meet her. Evenings were short, so meals waited until after dark when the filly was settled for the night, and at weekends, rain or shine, Joanna would pack a picnic lunch and off they would go for a long walk.

A phone call to the auctioneers had given her the address of Lucky's previous owners and she wrote off to them for details of the pony's background. We felt she couldn't have been running the Forest, as one of her major dislikes was walking through mud or water, both of which would have come fairly naturally to a Forester. Neither did she carry a brand. She led well, so it seemed that she had been handled regularly, but she showed a distinct will of her own with which Joanna coped quietly and firmly.

At last a letter arrived addressed to Joanna in a frail, laboriously written hand. It was a sad letter, expressing an old couple's joy that the little pony was well and happy. They had bought her as a foal at the previous year's sale, thinking that one day she would be there for their granddaughter. They lived near a town, however, and the field that they had been able to rent was sold for building. They had loved her dearly, but couldn't keep her. 'We watched you go,' said the letter. 'We waited until she went up into that nice box, and we knew she would be happy. Give her a kiss from me.'

Everyone loved her except the old gelding. We turned her out in a big paddock with two young geldings and the old boy, who took an instant dislike to having a female forced into his life.

'He's going to kill her,' reported an anxious tractor driver, who had rushed in to bang on the door, having just passed the gelding's paddock. We ran down to look and found the old chap furiously chasing Lucky away from the others, ears laid back and mouth ready to bite. She was much quicker on the turns, however, and was avoiding him easily. We watched to make sure she didn't get trapped in the corners, but she had too much sense to allow herself to be caught. He kept up the running battle for about a week, then we noticed the filly grazing on the outskirts of the group, unmolested. Several days later, as I passed their field, I realised that Lucky was nowhere to be seen. The geldings were in a group under the big chestnut tree, nose to tail, dozing and swishing their tails lazily, and it was several worried moments before I spotted her. She was in the middle of the bunch, standing with her head beneath the old gelding's chin while he obligingly sheltered her from the flies.

Chapter Eleven

THE beech trees around the Stud gave the first real sign that autumn was on the way. Just as their lovely delicate green leaves heralded each spring, their gradual change from green to gold and gold to russet told us that summer was over for yet another year. The days shortened, the sun shone with less warmth, and the leaves drifted down to fill the lanes with a thick soft carpet of brown, gold, red and yellow. Morning mists changed to rain more often than to sunshine, and the wind had more of a bite to it as it came rushing across the open downlands to sigh through the branches. His Lordship's barns bulged with sweet green hay, and his stores of corn and silage were safely gathered to fend for his stock over the winter. Already the stubble had been ploughed in and next year's cropping programme was under way.

Nature's harvest seemed to come overnight. Suddenly the hedgerows were swamped with lush blackberries and heavy clusters of red-black elderberries. Hazelnuts filled out their shells as they began to turn from green to brown, and the annual mushroom hunt began. Mushrooms grew in abundance on his Lordship's Estate, but never in the same field twice. From mid-autumn onwards, it seemed, every friendly greeting and murmured pleasantry exchanged between the locals was rounded off with a casual 'Seen any mushrooms yet?' Then, without warning, a tractor driver crossing a field or the dairyman checking his fences in the early misty morning would stumble across that year's crop, and the word would go around on the bush telegraph. Before first light,

each trying to be earlier than his neighbour, dark figures armed with buckets, baskets and bowls would converge on the mushroom field. They were not the flat, open field mushrooms that grew there, but lovely plump white buttons, with a soft pink underside just visible around their fat little stalks. They grew so thickly and froze so beautifully that a few mornings' steady picking could provide enough to last around until next mushroom time. Although the Good Lord had grown them, He did choose to do it on our employer's land, so we usually prepared a basket of the best and delivered them to Maisie for his Lordship's breakfast.

After the mushrooms, in order of importance, came the elderberries. Good elderberry wine is like a rich, heavy port of the most wonderful deep colour. Bad elderberry wine, of which we had made gallons, was still the same colour but with a bitter aftertaste. It was superb, however, for turning plain rabbit stew into a really exotic dish and very drinkable when mulled with nutmeg and oranges on a cold winter's evening. So, since good or bad it was never wasted, we could never resist making more when each year the berries hung plump, tempting and free. Cider was another experiment which turned out well. John had designed and made his own cider press which, with the help of the children and a small car jack, produced enough buckets of clear, golden apple juice to fill a forty gallon barrel. With the apples came the sloes: lovely silver-blue frosted berries hanging thick on the bough, so inviting and so impossible to eat! But they could transform the cheapest sherry into a thick, warming, liqueur-type drink, deep red in colour and with a rich, sweet-sour flavour that could take away the breath of the inexperienced. Best of all, it took only six weeks to mature, so was ready to drink by Christmas.

The apple pulp left over from the cider making was appreciated by all the animals, mixed in small quantities with their feed. The surplus we made into thick flat cakes, and froze them so that we would be able to add variety to their winter feeds. The elderberry pulp was pretty uninteresting stuff, but I decided to try some on Sadsac, having a natural aversion to wastage of any sort. I tipped a bit in his trough one evening, together with the potato peelings, barley and odd kitchen scraps, and watched as it vanished. Acceptable, it seemed. Bluebell couldn't reach the hedge behind the pig's pen, and there the weeds grew thickly, dandelion, hogweed, cow parsley and plantains. A rabbit's paradise. I dropped the bucket by the gate and hopped over, always quicker than going through, to gather a huge armful of mixed salads for Stanley and his wives. I'm sure they could smell it coming, as they were all standing expectantly on their hind legs, front feet braced against the wire, their brown splodged noses twitching in anticipation.

Stanley and the does had produced several families, averaging eight babies each litter. At first sight they were incredibly ugly. Fat, bald little pink-skinned creatures with wrinkled legs, pug noses and tightly screwed-up eyes. Their mothers kept them hidden from the world in the nesting boxes we had made, plucking great mounds of soft fur from their chests and bellies to cover up the baldness of their children until they had grown more presentable. Within a week or so the most advanced of the litter would be tumbling out of the nest to take a look at the great outdoors – a little fluffy white ball that would just fit into a cupped hand, with a tiny black tail on one side and two soft ears and a twitching nose on the other. Once mobile their mother had absolutely no peace, someone was always hungry. They would dive underneath and grab for a teat, rolling over onto their backs as they did so, like a mechanic under a car, and landing with a plop and a surprised expression as mother decided that enough was enough, and hopped away. They grew quickly and were soon transferred to the weaner cage, giving their mother time to relax and recover before Stanley came to visit again.

The cockerels were full sized now and far from lovable as I waded through them, trying to avoid the sharp beaks which threatened to tear lumps of flesh from my legs. I fed the rabbits and threw a handful of grain into the corner for the cockerels to create a diversion as I escaped through the door. All animals fed and content, now it was my turn, I decided: supper, hot chocolate and bed.

Next morning I stood in the kitchen doorway, staring puzzled at a grey mound half hidden in the grass at the edge of the path. I couldn't think what it was. It didn't move as I approached, but was obviously a small body of some kind. Then I realised. It was one of the Marans! A few paces on lay another one, and another – my heart missed a beat – they were all dead. I just couldn't believe it. They had been fine the night before, what could have killed them so quickly, and so quietly? I picked up the still warm, limp body and stroked the lovely speckled plumage. The eyes were half closed but looked strangely bright and from somewhere deep inside came a faint groan. Not quite dead, but nearly. I knelt by the others. They looked the same, no signs of violence, nothing. Then out of the corner of my eye I noticed the bucket of elderberry pulp. It was tipped on its side, practically empty.

The Marans weren't dying, they were stoned out of their minds! Legless. Nished as pewts. I sat one up and it rolled slowly over onto its side with a faint moan. Three paralytic cockerels. I left them heaped together for warmth while I hunted around the house for a cardboard box with high sides. After lining the bottom with straw I wedged the Marans in, side by side, in a sitting-up position, put the box in the dark shed out of the draught, and left them to sober up.

I went to look at Sadsac. He was snoring peacefully, but then he usually was, so whether he was likely to wake up with a hangover or not was difficult to tell. Bluebell had a pink beard, so had obviously been imbibing as well, but the constitution of a goat can withstand most things and she showed no ill effects. If this was an indication of the potency of our latest batch of wine we could be in for a pretty wild winter.

Then an idea crept into my mind. If it could do that to chickens, then what would it do to pheasants? At around 8.00 every morning at least seven or eight of these handsome game birds came wandering down past the kitchen window on their way from the woods to the horse shelters, where they went to find wasted grain. What if they were to come across a pile of alcoholic elderberries on the way? I saw myself gathering armfuls of blissfully anaesthetised pheasants, who would never know what had hit them. What a lovely way to go! Much better than being shot to pieces by his Lordship's shoot.

That evening I cautiously mentioned the idea to John.

'I think you'd be asking for trouble,' was his first reaction. 'Old misery guts wouldn't think twice about reporting you to his Lordship. Then where would we be? Marching down the road with our little spotted handkerchiefs over our shoulders.'

John and the gamekeeper had never quite seen eye to eye. My husband could see the sense of shooting for the pot, if you were hungry, but not killing for fun. Gamekeeping was a new idea for him, and his usual straightforward, open way of summing up the man's job had not endeared him to Walter Stone, who keepered for his Lordship. He had nodded understandingly as Walter had explained his job at their first meeting.

'I see, you look after the pheasants, so you have to shoot or trap anything that may harm them.'

'Ay,' Walter had scowled, 'foxes, stoats, weasels and such. An' then there's the vermin.'

'Vermin? You mean mice?'

'No, not mice! Crows, rooks, pigeons and rabbits. Anything what damages 'is Lordship's crops.'

'So during the year you kill everything that will harm the pheasants,' summed up John, 'and then you kill the pheasants?'

'Don't produce game 'nd crops fer vermin,' Walter had replied tartly. And thereafter he had limited his acquaintance with us to a curt nod in passing. I had to admit, John was right. Walter would take great pleasure in turning us in.

'On the other hand,' John moved the kettle over onto the hotplate of the Rayburn and reached for a couple of mugs, 'you've got to throw the stuff out somewhere. Where you put it is up to you, you don't need anyone's permission to throw it away.' He spooned hot chocolate powder into each mug and shook the kettle, encouraging it to boil. 'And if you happened to find the unfortunate pheasants first, well . . .'

A few evenings later, after dark, I crept stealthily along the paddock fence clasping my bowl of fermenting elderberries and keeping a sharp eye open for the gamekeeper. I knew well the route followed by the pheasants, and heaped tempting little snifters at random intervals along the way. The familiar trees creaked and groaned; it was creepy out there all by myself. The bushes spread clutching fingers at me as I passed, and the wet webs of countless spiders brushed my face and stuck to my eyelashes. Mice scuttled away from underfoot, and the barn owl shrieked a fearsome warning as he sailed past, a white shape swallowed by the misty rain. I scooped out the last of my bait with sticky fingers, wiped them clean on the cold wet grass, shaking off a slug in disgust, and turned for home and the warm light of the kitchen which I could just make out across the field.

I was half way over the paddock gate when I felt, rather than saw, the eyes. I knew they were following my every movement from the long grass at the edge of the field, and my heart skipped about ten beats before I heard the whine. I had no torch, and I could only guess at the exact spot, but surely, I told myself firmly, it must be a dog of some sort. I moved, heart pounding, towards the place from which I thought the sound had come. I was so nervous that my attempt at soothing encouragement came out as a frightened squeak, and that was followed by a full-blooded shriek as something nudged the back of my knee. The eyes were behind me. Dark and almond shaped, they were all that was visible on that cold, rainy night. The rest of the animal was black, and judging from the altitude of the eyes, stood at well over two and a half feet at the shoulder. As a gesture of friendship I offered a finger to sniff, and as a long hard muzzle was thrust into my hand I suddenly realised that I was stroking a Dobermann pinscher.

There is something very forbidding about a Dobermann. They have a silently lethal quality about them, and standing alone with one in the dark and the rain in the middle of a field, I wasn't too sure of my next move, until I felt my still sticky fingers being licked gently clean by a very long, warm, pink tongue. I put the hand safely into my pocket, moved quietly away a few yards and called him. He sat down and whined. I tried again and he followed a few steps, then with a sudden burst of confidence which shattered mine, he bounded towards me. I turned, shaking, and made once more for that friendly kitchen light and John, with my new find quietly trotting after me.

John rose to his feet quickly as I burst into the kitchen,

instantly misinterpreting my pale face and shaky dishevelled appearance. His startled gaze dropped from shoulder height, where he obviously expected Walter to appear, to just below my waist and his eyes widened further as the Dobermann wandered into the room.

'Ye Gods, Judy,' he relaxed slightly as I closed the door behind me, and stared at the dog as it sniffed its way around the room. 'Where did you find that?' (The question was asked in the same tone as I would have used to Joanna producing a frog from her pocket.)

'Actually, it found me.' I peeled off my wet clothes, reached for a warm towel from the rail on the Rayburn and rubbed myself dry. John handed me my gown automatically, still staring at the dog. He had the makings of a very fine animal. Black with rich tan markings, long powerful legs and almond shaped eyes set in a narrow head, which came to a very pronounced point at the top. His body was emaciated. The pin bones of his hips stuck out sharply and every rib and vertebra showed beneath the coat, which was remarkably glossy for his condition, even allowing for the rain. His claws

were very long and unworn so, we surmised, as he obviously hadn't walked very far, he must have been dumped. The next question was why? Had he savaged Grandma, killed sheep or simply failed as a guard dog? Probably we would never know, but one thing was certain, a meal wouldn't come amiss. We made up some porridge, added a good spoonful of Marmite and a stock cube, cooled it down with goats' milk and mixed in a couple of beaten eggs. He didn't even stop to sniff it, standing like a giraffe to eat, his long front legs splayed out on either side of the basin, pushing it around the kitchen in his efforts to get the very last drop.

'We'd better phone the police,' decided John, 'just in case someone is looking for him.' He ran a hand bumpily along the dog's back. 'But I must say, whoever it is he belongs to, they don't deserve to find him and he doesn't deserve to be found.'

PC Watts, our local bobby, was only too pleased to leave him with us while they tried to trace his owners. 'Last thing I need', he declared down the phone, 'is a ravenous Dobermann of unknown origin. Probably belongs to one of them poachers I've been after. They've been nickin' 'is Lordship's pheasants again, y'know.'

I gulped guiltily and thrust an elderberry-stained hand back into the pocket of my robe. 'Anyway,' he was saying, 'you be careful how you handle him, and I'll let you know if anyone reports him missing.'

We cleared a corner of the kitchen, spread a couple of old coats out to make a comfortable bed, and left the dog to sniff around and settle quietly, while we retired to the old settee in the lounge to toast our toes in front of the fire and watch the late news on TV. Ten minutes later there were three of us there. With a full tummy and a warm fire our lethal-looking visitor had been transformed into an oversized puppy with an overpowering desire to sit on our knees!

Morning dawned as grey and misty as the previous evening had been, and I peered from our bedroom window, eagerly searching the edges of the paddock for recumbent pheasant forms. Nothing. They were usually well on their way to the feed troughs by now, but nothing stirred in the long wet grass and there were no dark tracks to show that they had passed. I pulled on wellies and a warm coat and, followed by a well-breakfasted Dobermann who was sticking to his meal ticket like a leech, I wandered casually down to remove the heaps of berries before Walter tripped over them. But not a berry remained. Pheasant tracks led from the wood to where the berries had been, and then back again into the thick tangle of bushes at the edge of the trees. I sighed. Another brilliant idea had failed.

I was well through most of my morning chores when the Dobermann rose suddenly from where he had been lying on the threshold, his hackles raised and his eyes intent on something across the field. The low, rumbling growl rose gradually in volume until it erupted suddenly into a deep, echoing bay, which was emitted with such force that his front feet came clean off the ground. Following his gaze, I could see a man standing in the field. Then I saw another, and another. All in a line facing the wood. His Lordship's shooting party!

Very soon the whole coppice was filled with the shouts and whistles of the beaters. They whooped and yelled, banging the tree trunks with their sticks and shaking plastic bags, while labradors galloped to and fro, sniffing and scuffling noisily through the fallen leaves. From the topmost branches pigeons and rooks flapped hastily away and from the smaller bushes blackbirds and robins darted hither and thither, twittering in alarm. But deep in the heart of the big bramble clumps the pheasants snored contentedly. Lost in the drunken stupor which followed their previous night's binge, the whole commotion passed unnoticed. Rabbits broke cover and thudded away to be quickly swallowed up by the long grass, ignored by the guns who were waiting for a better prize. The Dobermann and I sat side by side in the doorway and watched with interest. The figures of the beaters could now be plainly seen as they came to the edge of the wood, face to face with the waiting line of guns, who so far hadn't fired a single shot. The tall wiry figure of his Lordship came trotting up the line, shooting stick waving from one hand as he enquired testily for the whereabouts of his gamekeeper. This most unfortunate of men stood dejectedly to one side as his professional capabilities went under review, and the beaters leaned against trees trying not to listen to the embarrassing conversation taking place between his Lordship and their immediate superior. Eventually the whole party drifted away across the fields towards the next coppice, and half an hour later a fairly continuous volley of shots signalled a reprieve, at least for Walter.

By the end of the week we had heard nothing from the police regarding the rightful owners of our new companion, but one thing was sure – Mutt, as John had impolitely named the Dobermann, was happy! His forbidding appearance concealed a sweet, gentle nature that desperately sought warmth and affection, and he repaid it one hundredfold. A strong bond of friendship developed between us over those first few weeks, and together we uncovered a whole new world.

Mutt was obviously a town dog, and through his eyes I got a second chance to discover those things which, up to then, I had considered familiar or just taken for granted. I watched him as he studied Bluebell. She stood knee deep in the long grass, grazing steadily, tearing off mouthful after mouthful of the lush, green blades with a regular upward pull of her head. Mutt stared, thought about it, then lowered his head and gave a few experimental tugs. His teeth, however, were not designed for grazing and only a few wisps came away. These were thoroughly chewed and eventually swallowed. He concentrated on Bluebell's technique for a few more minutes then tried again, this time with more success, and before long he was away, grazing contentedly alongside her, legs splayed, head jerking. Bumblebees fascinated him, grasshoppers made him sneeze. He longed to play with the chickens, but when he capered towards them, stumpy tail wagging, a big friendly grin on his face, they rather unsportingly shot into the air squawking and scattered in all directions. Squirrels could vanish. He knew that for a fact. They went in one side of a tree and they didn't come out of the other. Pheasants were the most fun, they could take off almost vertically if you were quick enough, but people did tend to shout quite loudly when that happened.

Mutt disliked getting into a car and flatly refused to go upstairs. His tail stump would sink, his ears droop and he would carefully stay out of arm's reach until he was certain that any such suggestion had been abandoned. Obviously they brought back memories he wished to forget. When I managed, at last, to entice him into the car I took him to my favourite woods for a walk, keeping him on a lead as I wasn't too sure he would stay near enough to be under control. It was the first time we had been away from the Stud together, and he became more and more excited at the fresh smells and different surroundings. The footpath crossed a big, empty field, and as I shut the gate behind us his excitement increased. He leapt around like a puppy and, jumping up, he put his paws on my shoulders and looked straight into my face with shining eyes and an expression which said so plainly, 'Let me go, oh, go on – let me go!'

I let him go, and after a few ecstatic bounds around me he shot away like a bullet and in no time had vanished over the horizon. Well, that's that, I told myself dejectedly, you woman of very little brain, you've lost him. It must have been a full five minutes before a very fast-moving black dot appeared over the hill to my left and came zooming down the steep turf-covered slopes. He moved like a leopard, long effortless bounds which covered the ground with a speed which was deceptively fast. He threw himself down in the grass beside me, flanks heaving, tongue lolling from a wide, panting mouth which curved unmistakably in a contented grin. I felt as if I had just successfully thrown a boomerang.

Mutt loved the water. Like a child he would go out of his way to walk through even the smallest puddle, but although he would splash and paddle in the little streams which cut down through the woods, he could never quite pluck up the courage to swim. We picked blackberries together, I picked the high ones and he picked the low ones, sniffing them out and gently pulling them from the stalk with lips curled back, to chew them with great enjoyment. I had to stop taking him mushrooming, because he soon realised what I was looking for and would pounce on them with disastrous results. His sense of smell was acute. And Mutt loved a fight. Stump wagging, he would return my shoves and punches by leaning in with his shoulder and grabbing my arm with ferocious snarls. He rarely left a mark, but if by some accident he did make me shout he would immediately stop and give me a good licking. He followed me everywhere, and in the evenings when we settled down for an hour before bed, his place was right next to my chair with his chin on my feet.

Chapter Twelve

FARMING on a large scale is highly mechanised, and his Lordship's farms were extremely well equipped on the arable side. The shepherd's life has changed little over the years, sheep being basically the same and needing the same sort of care and handling. The crook and the dog were still Mac's main tools, and the introduction of preventative medicines and vaccines, while improving the health and life expectancy of the flock, made more work for the flock master. The shepherd sitting on the hill, smoking his pipe and watching his sheep is a rare sight these days, and I knew of more than one shepherd on tranquillisers!

The dairies lent themselves more towards mechanisation and his Lordship's herd was milked in a sparkling clean, modern parlour. A computer delivered the correct amount of concentrated ration to each cow as she entered, milk went straight from cow to bulk tank via pipelines, and the milking clusters automatically removed themselves from the cow when her milk had been given. At the end of each milking session high pressure hoses cleaned away every last speck of mud and muck and sent it swooshing down into a dark, evil smelling lagoon, where it lay until ready to be dispersed onto the land. This could also be done at the touch of a button, whereupon a powerful pump propelled the liquid slurry out along a pipeline into the fields where it was forced at great pressure through a nozzle which sprayed it, like a gigantic lawn sprinkler, over a wide area.

The stables were the least mechanised of all. The boxes

were mucked out each day with fork, shovel and wheel-barrow, and the yards kept spotlessly clean and tidy by much laborious sweeping with besom brooms. The horses were groomed by hand, although electric grooming kits did exist, and were led out daily on foot, as it was not the general policy of his Lordship to have the brood mares and stallions ridden. Some of them were ridden very occasionally. John rode the Stallion whenever he had time, and also the big chestnut stallion that Debbie looked after, but the majority were schooled only in the ways of the showring.

Now sixth sense is a funny thing. Some people seem to have it and some people don't. I think John must have had it when he came to find me one morning as I was brushing out boxes. His face wore a slightly worried look. 'Go and give Debbie a hand, would you, my love? You may be able to reach the parts that she can't.' Affectionately nicknamed Shandy, Debbie's stallion was a solid sixteen hands high while Debbie just about made five feet in her wellies.

'Had a phone call from his Lordship, he's coming to ride at ten this morning, so we must have Shandy looking his best.' John looked worried again. 'I just hope that stallion behaves himself, he doesn't get ridden much these days.'

Debbie was standing in the manger, lovingly brushing out Shandy's golden mane when I arrived. The stallion had his head lowered and his eyes shut, blissfully lapping up every minute of her attention. His coppery coat gleamed and his mane and tail shone like spun gold. 'If you could give me a hand with his bridle,' Debbie waved a hand towards the pile of tack in the corner, 'he always puts his head up in the air, and he knows I can't reach.'

By five to ten he was ready, and Debbie craftily removed the haynet before he could shower himself with hayseeds and spoil the effect. John peered over the half-door and smiled his approval, then hurried away as his Lordship's Land Rover drew into the yard. He was soon back with his Lordship, who was as immaculately dressed as always, this time in expensively tailored jacket and breeches, leather riding boots and a smart cap, which had obviously never had a close encounter with the ground. John slid back the bolt and pushed open the door as our employer acknowledged us briefly and watched with a critical eye as Debbie led Shandy out to stand by the mounting block. As his Lordship slid into the saddle and moved the big stallion across the yard it seemed obvious that Shandy was in a tractable mood and John's anxious expression faded. His Lordship was, after all, an extremely good horseman, and there really was very little cause for concern. As he rode past his Land Rover, he gestured towards his labrador, which was leaping excitedly around on the back seat.

'I'll take him with me if you would just be so good as to open the door.' He glanced at his watch. 'I'm going to the dairy, so I shall probably be away for a couple of hours.'

It was probably sixth sense which told me to ring Jim and tell him that his Lordship was on his way, but fate intervened by way of a phone call for John, and then I just forgot. The dairy could be reached by riding directly across the fields and through a small wood, and it was this route that his Lordship chose to follow that day. It was a bright winter's morning, and they looked a picture as the big chestnut stallion paced proudly away across the grass, the yellow labrador coursing to and fro, stopping to sniff awhile and then bounding after his master as horse and rider were swallowed up by the dark trees of the little copse. Most of the gates on the Estate were fitted with special 'hunt' latches, which made them easy to open and close from horseback, but the little gate on the far side of the wood had a normal type of clasp, which was stiff and difficult to close. His Lordship manoeuvred the stallion easily through the narrow gateway, but found it necessary to dismount to close it properly.

Doubtless it was the stallion's sixth sense that made him fidget as he impatiently waited for his Lordship to remount, but his sense of impending disaster was not transmitted to his rider, as his Lordship set course for the dairy buildings which could be seen on the far side of the field. Neither did Jim seem to have any sort of premonition as, down in his spotless parlour, he took one last look around and pressed the button which activated the slurry disposal system. Slurry travelling at speed down a pipe makes an unmistakable noise, and the nozzle at the end of the line was aimed towards that corner of the field nearest the wood. The force with which it erupted made evasive action impossible, for although the Arab is remarkably fleet of foot it cannot fly, and vertical take-off would really have been the only escape route.

Five minutes later Jim looked out across the yard and his eyes widened in disbelief. Cantering into view came a shining green horse, ridden by a wildly gesticulating green man. He rubbed his eyes and looked away, but when he looked back they were still there, and making straight for him too. It was the green labrador that brought the first stirrings of recognition, and when he moved out into the yard and downwind of the trio the truth really hit him. Well, as Jim pointed out to me later, what can you say in a situation like that? 'Good morning' seemed inadequate, even if he had been given time to say it.

The stallion was hastily housed in a calving box and Bert summoned to conduct his Lordship homewards by car. On the phone, Jim, with his Lordship at his elbow, had been very discreet and merely requested prompt assistance as his Lordship had met with an accident while out riding. Unaware of the nature of the emergency, therefore, Bert arrived in his own car and immediately wished that he hadn't. 'Fair made my eyes water,' he confided to us later, when we arrived to collect Shandy. It took many hours of scrubbing to get the Arab clean, by which time we and his Lordship at last had something in common! It was quite a while before we felt nice to be near, and by the way his Lordship's aftershave heralded his presence on his next visit, I guess he felt the same.

By the end of October Sadsac had reached part three of the garden, and we had to face the fact that in the overall plan of things, step four was the freezer. He was no longer the endearing little piglet we had brought home in a sack, but he was a friendly fellow, and although I realised that his squeals of delight in seeing me were wholly brought about by the bucket I carried, it was with a sick feeling of treachery that I dialled the number of the Farmers' Meat Corporation. A time was set for 7.00 am the following Wednesday, which meant a very early start. It was over an hour's drive to the abattoir. As John had to be at the Stud by 7.00 am, the part of villain fell to me, and my heart was very heavy as I pulled on my multiple layers at 5.00 am that cold, dark October morning.

Despite the fact that it was three hours too early for breakfast, our appearance in the brightly lit doorway of the kitchen brought an immediate excited squeal from Sadsac, and at his signal the chickens hurled themselves from their perches, zigzagging across the garden and getting under our feet, while Bluebell started calling loudly and insistently. We had borrowed a van for the morning, as Sadsac could have demolished the little Renault without really trying too hard, and I didn't fancy driving forty miles with nothing but a dog guard between me and a cross pig. John had made a ramp that fitted up to the floor of the van, which was backed up to the gateway of section three. I don't think pigs have very good eyesight, their ears tend to get in the way a lot, but Sadsac's sense of smell was pretty keen, and he could pinpoint a bucket at one hundred yards. He wasn't at all bothered that his breakfast was at the top of the ramp instead of in his usual trough, and he trotted up into the van with surprising agility for one so plump. We quickly shut the doors and made them fast before he realised he had been short-rationed and then, after a commiserating squeeze of my hand, John opened the gate and watched us glumly until we were out of sight.

It was both dark and foggy, and big puddles lay along the

lanes full of wet slippery fallen leaves. I could feel no move-ment from the back of the van, so Sadsac had presumably burrowed under the straw and gone back to sleep. He was obviously feeling a lot more relaxed than I was. It was a winding route and my watch showed 6.50 am as I drove through the gates of the abattoir. The lights in the reception area blazed, and already lorries were pulling away, as the drivers delivered their live cargoes and turned homewards, with the thought of breakfast uppermost in their minds. I backed the van up to the gate and tiptoed away to find someone before Sadsac woke up. I felt the longer he slept the happier he would be and the happier I would be. I'm not quite sure what I had expected, but I was met by a kindly man of around sixty, with a gentle smile and a quiet way about him. His office was warm and inviting, with picture postcards around the walls and a desk piled high with paper-work. He rummaged in a drawer for the right pad of forms, wrote down my name and address and issued a tattoo number which, he explained, would be given to the pig so that we got the right one back – they had several hundred there that morning.

'Don't you worry about him, my dear,' he gave me a reassuring smile, 'no one's going to hurt him.'

This struck me as a very incongruous remark until I realised that it was made in all sincerity, and as he showed me the other pigs all wandering about contentedly in the roomy straw-littered lairage it was quite obvious that they were under no stress at all.

'Let's get him out then, shall we?' He led the way back to the van, undid the safety rope and opened the doors wide. For a moment I thought I had somehow lost him, not a pig to be seen, but my companion wasn't easily fooled. He pointed knowingly to a piece of straw that was rising and falling slowly in time with the deep sleeping breaths of a contented Sadsac. He was completely buried and snoring softly.

'Come on, then. Wakey, wakey.' The little man hopped

nimbly into the back of the van, and as the pig rose sleepily to his feet he gave him a brisk swat with some instrument he was carrying and, hey presto, the indignant Sadsac was tattooed and waddling, ears pricked, towards the piggy sounds coming from around the corner. I drove away with the feeling that, although I still felt a miserable traitor, we had done our best for him. Every living being has to pass from this life at some time and the natural way is rarely painless. A short life and a happy one was the only way to look at it, if we were to continue to be self-supporting. None of us liked to think too deeply about that stage which had to come between prime meat on the hoof and meat in the pot.

The cockerels were another problem in as much as they now weighed around fifteen pounds and sported strong beaks and spurs.

'Why don't you ask Peter to do it?' suggested James. Peter, apprenticed to Walter, the gamekeeper, had doubtless been skilled in the art of despatching small animals and birds from a very early age. 'He's always looking for a way to earn a bit extra, and it's the sort of thing he wouldn't think twice about.'

John went off to ring him, and came back five minutes later wearing a relieved expression. 'That's settled then, he'll come each Saturday morning and deal with anything that's ready to go, rabbits and cockerels, and we can prepare them and stick them in the freezer.'

We soon became quite expert at plucking cockerels and skinning rabbits. We had an abortive attempt at curing the skins, but most of the fur fell out, which rather defeated the object of the whole thing, so they were hastily buried. We had never seen such birds as the cockerels. Plucked, cleaned and trussed ready for the table they averaged around twelve pounds each and carved like a young turkey. The children approved wholeheartedly of this side of self-sufficiency, but strangely enough insisted that the rabbits had to be portioned before cooking. Apparently it was fine to eat a roast chicken that looked like a chicken, but not a rabbit that looked like a rabbit.

We had cheated a little by sending part of our pork to be professionally cured, reasoning that it was less expensive than doing it unsuccessfully ourselves. Bacon, therefore, came as thick rashers cut with a knife, and Mr Boyes had been dead right about the nasturtium seeds and apple rings – we wished I had pickled more. The freezer became more and more laden as we stowed away rabbit, poultry, bacon and pork. Like busy squirrels we packed in mushrooms, blackberries and sliced apples in addition to the vegetables from our now very fertile garden. Joanna delighted in taking rabbit pie and home-made pickles to school for lunch, and used us as a basis for many a colourful essay. One sentence particularly sticks in my mind. 'If it moves, we eat it, if it grows, we pickle it.' Parents' evenings became acutely embarrassing.

Chapter Thirteen

'THIS animal never stops scratching.' John gave Mutt a shove with his toe, as the dog – snuffling loudly – enthusiastically hunted a flea down his flank and under his belly. 'Have you tried louse powder?'

I had. Several times. But it didn't seem to make a scrap of difference. It seemed he could never relax. As soon as we settled down in the evenings the constant nibbling, licking and scratching began.

'I think we should take him to the vet,' decided John. 'Perhaps there's some sort of shampoo that would stop it.'

The following evening we joined the little group of people sitting glumly around the vet's waiting room. There were three vets on duty, and they were working their way steadily through the list of patients. One man in a white coat came out of his little consulting room and stopped short at the sight of Mutt. Standing thirty inches high at the shoulder, he was a pretty impressive sight. The man smiled wanly. 'I bet I get him,' I heard him mutter to the receptionist, glancing around the room and mentally ticking off the remaining patients in threes. And he did. Mutt followed us obediently into the ante-room and allowed himself to be thoroughly inspected. As the vet worked his way from nose to tail he relaxed noticeably, for Mutt enjoyed any kind of attention and was far from aggressive. He was still much too thin, but had put on pounds over the last few weeks and I was very proud of him. The vet straightened up and gave him a pat.

'Hang on a minute, will you? I'd just like my partner to see this.' He hurried out and came back with a dark, serious-looking, middle-aged man.

'Jim Gordon,' he introduced himself briefly and held out a hand. 'So what have we got here, Tim?' He stroked Mutt's elegantly pointed head and peered closely into his face. 'Oh, yes,' his voice was very quiet, 'classic symptoms. See here,' he traced a line around the dog's eyes, 'completely gone, and it's gone down the neck and between his legs here.' He took a piece of skin and rolled it gently between his finger and thumb. 'That's not very elastic either.' He stood back with a sigh. 'What a damn shame, super dog too. Isn't it always the same.'

By this time my heart was beginning to thump and a nasty little knot of worry was weaving around in my stomach. Tim glanced at me sympathetically.

'Demodectic mange,' he said simply.

'Mange? Well, surely there's a shampoo for that?'

He shook his head. 'Not this sort. You see,' he went on, sitting down next to Mutt and pulling playfully at the soft ears, 'every animal has the particular mite that causes this. All dogs have it, you and I have it. It's just that one dog in ninety doesn't have any immunity to it like most of us do. They pick up the mite from their mother when they suckle as pups, that's why we see it on the head first, you see how the skin is bare around his eyes and muzzle – he's got no whiskers where he's continually scratching. It's not a case of getting rid of the mite, you can't. It's a case of providing an immunity and we can't do that either. It will get worse and he'll just scratch himself to pieces.'

My eyes were beginning to fill with tears. I knew what he was going to say.

'Most of these cases are put down in their first year.' He shifted around uncomfortably. 'Well, he's really lucky to have lasted so long.'

To everyone's acute embarrassment the tears silently overflowed, streaming down my cheeks, mixed feelings of sorrow and anger in my heart. Lucky to have lasted so long. Lasted through nearly two years of neglect and starvation to reach a brief few weeks of affection and understanding. I had been so pleased with the way he had been putting on weight, and so happy to share his enthusiasm for life and all the new experiences that had previously been denied him, that I had missed the now obvious signs of trouble. Looking at him now through my tears I could see the whiskerless muzzle, and the thinning hair on his ears and chest. For the first time I noticed the discomfort showing in his eyes and realised the real reason for the crusty discharge from their corners, which I thought would come right with the sort of care I could give him.

'I suppose I could try an injection of Ivomec,' Tim was saying. 'It's actually a new cattle wormer, but it's supposed to have a very long-lasting effect on most parasites. I suppose it could work on the mite.'

I knew he was clutching at straws. I turned miserably to John, who sat holding my hand tightly, not knowing what to say. 'Perhaps . . .' The tears started again, making it difficult to speak. 'Perhaps, while we are here, it would be best for Mutt if . . . if we . . .' I couldn't say any more, and searched around desperately for a hanky.

John found his and placed it firmly in my hand. 'Give him a chance,' he said quietly, 'it's a long shot, but give it a chance.'

Mutt took the injection calmly and we drove home in silence. On the way we stopped at the path through the woods where I had first let Mutt run free. He dashed joyfully away, bumbling over the grass like some enormous black daddy-long-legs. If he had been hurt or sick I could have accepted it, but he was so alive, so full of fun. Give it a week, Tim had said, if it's going to do any good there should be some improvement in a week.

It was a very miserable seven days, and Mutt was no better. John had to be away with one of the mares on the day of our second appointment with Tim, and I forced myself into a reasonably calm state of mind as I drove. I prayed that someone would have thought of an answer, perhaps something new had come to light that very week, something in its experimental stage even. I prayed for anything, just anything. Tim had suggested a time just before main surgery, probably guessing that he would have a tearful female to deal with again — not the best advertisement in a crowded surgery waiting room. He ushered us straight into his consulting room, taking in at a glance the obvious deterioration in Mutt's condition since the week before.

He shook his head slowly. 'No better, eh? Damn!' He squatted down beside Mutt and got a big, slurpy lick on the nose. 'Such a super temperament for a Dobe.' He tugged an ear thoughtfully, stood back looking at Mutt for a minute, and then heaved himself up onto the edge of the examination table and sat there swinging his long legs pensively.

'There was this American student,' he said suddenly, 'I met him at a conference. He reckoned that in time all these skin disorders can be cleared up with thyroid tablets. He reckoned it's used a lot in the States, but we've not really tried it here. It might take up to a year, but it's not expensive. Do you want to give it a go?'

He doesn't often give a direct answer to a prayer, so when He does it takes a moment or two to sink in — but there it was, something new, in its experimental stage here, but a remedy used with confidence in America. Tim didn't need an answer. 'The dose will take a bit of working out.' He stared at Mutt. 'I wonder what he weighs. Oh, well, here goes.' He began to rummage in a cupboard, came out with a pair of bathroom scales and solemnly weighed himself. 'Good Lord, I need more exercise — come on, old lad,' and before either of us knew what was happening he had hoisted a very surprised and slightly embarrassed looking Mutt into his arms and was back on the scales again.

'Whew! When he's in proper condition he's going to be gi-normous.'

He put Mutt back on the floor, grabbed a pen and started to make a few muttered calculations. 'Well,' he said at last, 'he might rattle a bit. He's going to need ten a day and I'll give you a course of anti-irritant pills as well, just to try and break the scratching habit.'

The little car flew home. We stopped again on the way, at Mutt's wood, and as we walked I said another prayer – thanks for such a quick reply and for the hope we now had.

Each morning Mutt got a pill sandwich. Lots of margarine on two slices of bread with his eleven pills stuck firmly into it. He began to expect this daily snack, and within a week the scratching had almost stopped.

'Ye gods,' exclaimed John, 'he's grown a moustache!' And it did look like it. We had got so used to him without whiskers he looked quite comical with them – like a teenager trying to look grown up. Two weeks from the start of his treatment I took him back to the surgery. Tim was talking to an elderly man at the reception desk as I walked in with Mutt. He glanced at us briefly and then stopped mid-sentence, his mouth open, and looked back at us in disbelief.

'My God. He looks marvellous!' he hissed in a stage-type whisper, then apologised hastily to his client, who turned and stared at us curiously. When he had gone Tim threw open the door to his little consulting room. 'Bring him in, bring him in. What a dramatic change!' His examination was brief and his smile broad as he finished.

'Keep on with the tablets?' I suggested.

'Hell, yes. I daren't change a thing. Quite honestly I don't understand why it's happening, but as it is let's not question it!'

And so the moustache grew thick and the bald ears became covered in soft, silky hair. Mutt's coat gleamed with good health and his muscles developed. Within one month Mutt was an impressive sight, and I saw more than one car drive into the yard and out again without stopping!

Chapter Fourteen

THE snow came suddenly, fine, soft wet flakes, which settled quickly over the surrounding countryside. With it came the wind, blowing the snow into great drifts which filled the hollows and built up in the lanes until, in some places, it became level with the tops of the hedges. It sifted through closed windows, and piled up against the doors of the house and buildings. As we struggled, heads down against the horizontal stinging snow, to carry hurdles and plastic-covered windbreaks to protect the little shed the wind came screaming through the beech trees to pluck them from our numb fingers and hurl them like kites into the air.

The goats, hating to be wet more than anything, huddled miserably in the furthermost corner of their pens with snow-frosted beards. Stanley and his wives seemed unworried by the cold, although the water bowls in their cages repeatedly froze solid within a few hours. At last the wind dropped and the storm passed, leaving us in a bright, silent world of white. Joanna and Lucky played in the snowdrifts, both revelling in the sheer joy of being young and being together. The filly, warm in her thick winter coat, frolicked and rolled, springing up to buck, sidekick and leap away through the knee-high snow, as Joanna cavorted after her, throwing snowballs and falling down until they looked like snowhorse and snowgirl. The boys built an enormous snowman and took photographs of each other jumping out of the bedroom window into snowdrifts. As the snow built up the electricity lines came down, and with them went our lights and power for the freezer.

'Don't worry,' John reassured me, 'it'll be fine for several days as long as you don't open it too often.'

So we lit candles and sat around the fire writing Christmas cards and shopping lists. The milk lorries couldn't get through, so milk from his Lordship's dairy was freely distributed throughout the village, while poor Jim struggled with generators and frozen pipes in a sub-zero, open-ended milking parlour. At last the snow-blowers came through, sending pillars of fine white spray to land at the verge side and giving access to the heavy snowploughs which cleared a deep, single lane. They were closely followed by the milk tanker, signalling the end of unlimited free milk for all. The main roads were clear and we were soon more or less back to normal, with thoughts of Christmas brought even nearer by the glittering, frosted snowscape around us.

Christmas in the countryside comes later than in the cities. While the person living in town is besieged by plastic Christmas trees and tinsel, coloured baubles and Christmas cards from practically the last day of the July sales, we only wake up to the season when the first carols come to us over the radio. The children start to glow with that special bright, excited look that can only mean Christmas, and the Estate workers start to patrol his Lordship's woodlands at night to discourage Christmas tree thieves. Then is the time to note which holly bushes have the best berries and to remember where we saw that big clump of mistletoe growing.

Christmas trees came with the compliments of his Lordship, and when I arrived back from shopping ours was leaning against the side of the shed waiting for us. I was busily putting away the groceries when the gamekeeper popped his head around the door, wearing his annual smile. 'She's enjoyin' that,' he grinned, dropping a pair of limp pheasants on the kitchen table, and banging the snow from his boots.

I looked at him, puzzled. 'Who's enjoying what?'

'That there goat.' He jerked his head towards the open back door. Bluebell was tucking into the Christmas tree as only a goat could. Most of one side had already been completely trimmed back to the trunk, and she jumped guiltily as I sprang at her from the doorway, arms flailing like an enraged spider. The chuckles from the gamekeeper subsided as she danced away from me and leapt gracefully onto the bonnet of his truck, shaking her head and tempting me to come and chase her. I had long ago learned the futility of such attempts, so using my well-practised guile I took advantage of her greedy nature to coax her into the shed and shut the door on her.

Walter was soon pacified with a man-sized sample of our sloe sherry, and as the level of the thick warming liquid in the glass sank, so his spirits rose. He was half way through a long story about poachers and how he'd almost caught them, when he happened to glance out of the window. Half a dozen plump and beautiful cock pheasants were wandering down casually along the side of the paddock, picking here and there at some especially tasty morsel and then carrying on in an unhurried fashion.

'An' that,' he suddenly interrupted himself, leaping to his feet and pointing a shaking, enraged finger at the unsuspecting birds, 'that takes some explainin'! When we went through that covert a few weeks back there weren't a pheasant to be seen. Where was they? That's what I'd like to know.' The memory of it all came flooding back to him as he glared after the retreating birds, and in the tenseness of the moment he rather foolishly drained his glass in one gulp. This set off a bout of coughing which made his eyes stream and caused him to fight for breath. He glared at the empty glass. 'Gaw, that's some stuff, ennit?'

'A top-up?' I hastily filled his glass.

'I'm out all weathers,' he went on miserably, wiping his eyes, 'all hours. When most folks is out enjoyin' themselves I'm out there lookin' after me birds. And is it appreciated?

Not by some it's not!' He glowered towards the coppice, scene of his embarrassment.

'I can't understand it. They was there when I fed 'em the night before, then overnight they vanish. I'd 'ave said poachers, but now they're back!' He turned to me. 'You seen 'em?' he demanded, verifying the fact that they weren't ghostly apparitions haunting him from the past. 'Large as life, they've come back.'

I murmured something soothing.

'Nature's a funny taskmaster,' he was saying. 'You just think you've got it all worked out and she changes 'er mind. Proves she's a woman.'

I picked up the beautifully feathered brace from the table and hung them carefully on a hook behind the larder door. 'Well, these are a credit to you, I must say. Couldn't wish for better pheasants than that. Will you thank his Lordship for me?'

Walter cautiously drained his glass, set it down on the table and reached for his coat. 'Aye, that I will. We had a pretty good bag in the end.' He was looking more cheerful. 'His Lordship was well pleased with the way it all turned out.' He inclined his head towards the larder, where the birds dangled dejectedly from a binder twine necktie. 'That's two good 'uns you've got there,' he frowned sternly. 'Don't you spoil 'em in the cooking, now.'

Goodwill to all men, a small voice inside me warned quickly. 'I'll do my best not to. Happy Christmas to you and your family.'

'Yes, well, Happy Christmas to you too.' And he went off, whistling tunelessly.

John made a good job of the tree, turning its bald side to the wall and fitting it into a hollowed log to disguise the stripped bark. The children decorated it and piled mysterious-looking parcels around its base. One of the home-cured hams, which had been hanging in the pantry since the pig had reached section three of the garden, was taken down and put to soak.

The Rayburn was kept stoked up to bake relays of mince pies for the friends, neighbours and carol singers who would shortly be calling. One of my Christmas presents had come early in the news that I could keep Mutt. According to PC Watts, he had been reported missing by his owners, who had lost him on a day out in the country. They lived in a small town flat, freely acknowledged that such a large dog had been a mistake for them and were more than happy to give him to a good home. We had parted with both of the kids, who had gone to a farm where they would eventually be part of a team of goats producing milk to rear calves.

Sitting around the fire on Christmas Eve, with our mugs of hot mulled wine, we went back over our first year of self-sufficiency – or self-deficiency, as John was apt to call it. From the moment we had knocked on Mr Mills's front door, it seemed, we had been caught up in the old country way of living. We now produced our own meat in the way of chicken, pork, rabbit and bacon. Eggs and milk, cheese and wine, preserves and chutneys loaded the shelves in our little larder.

'So what are you old fogeys planning for next year?' asked Richard, cheekily, peering through the rich red wine in his glass at the leaping flames.

'Can't we get a cow?' suggested James, hopefully. He was still not completely convinced about goats' milk.

'Not enough land,' sighed John, wistfully. 'Wouldn't it be great to have a nice little Jersey house cow?'

'Fresh cream and eclairs,' James was ahead of him now, 'clotted cream fudge, scones and cream . . .'

'That would mean gallons of skimmed milk,' pointed out Joanna, 'so we could keep more pigs and I could raise some calves.'

'I'd like to keep bees,' went on John. 'They're really fascinating.'

'What would you like to do, Mum?' Joanna gave me a nudge.

I'd been secretly thinking about what I'd like to do for some time. 'Sheep,' I announced. 'I would really like to have a flock of sheep . . .'

'That's a good idea,' agreed James with enthusiasm. 'Roast lamb and mint sauce.'

'. . . and milk them,' I continued bravely. 'I want to make ewes' milk cheese and yoghurt.'

There was a sudden lull in the conversation.

'I just knew it wouldn't be simple,' declared James at last. 'Why do you two always have to be crazy?'

'And I want to spin the wool, and make our own clothes,' I went on, unabashed. 'Did you know that wool from five sheep can clothe a large family?'

'Not the way you knit,' grinned John.

'Well, someone else can knit it,' I retorted. 'After all, if I'm doing all the lambing, milking, dairy work and spinning, I shall have no time to *knit*.'

Joanna gave a deep sigh. 'I worry about you,' she confided. 'How am I going to cope with you when you're old?'

John gave her a startled look. 'How do you mean?'

'Well, you can't go on for ever. You've got to be realistic about it – but you won't. I mean, you'll still be doing crazy things when you're ninety – falling over and getting up again – you'll both be difficult, I know you will!'

The wine's gone to her head I told myself, we're not that bad.

'When we are ninety,' John pointed out reasonably, 'you can hit us with your walking stick, 'cause you'll be sixty-one.'

Joanna frowned at him. 'I was being serious.'

'Well, there's a lot of things I want to do before I'm ninety,' I assured her. 'So the sooner we start the better.'

John had been glancing through the page of the *Gazette*. 'What sort of sheep?' he asked, rubbing his nose thoughtfully.

'Jacobs. I thought if we crossed Jacobs with a milk-breed ram, perhaps a Friesland, we would get good wool, plenty of milk and hardy lambs.'

'Mmmm. We could call them Frejacs,' suggested my husband.

James and Richard exchanged glances.

'They're going to do it,' mourned James, burying his face in his hands. 'We're going to be drinking lousy sheep's milk.'

'And wearing hand-knitted Y-fronts,' agreed his brother.

John stabbed a finger at the paper. 'Here we are. I thought I remembered seeing something about Jacobs. The Society plans to hold its sale next year in Barfield for the first time. Be about August, I expect.'

'That's wonderful! It gives us eight months to save up a bit of capital.'

John folded his newspaper carefully, reached for his wine and drank deeply. 'If anyone asks what I would like for last-minute Christmas presents,' he stated quietly, 'I would very much like to stock up on underpants.'

The telephone shrilled loudly, shattering the peace with its insistent tone. I looked at my watch. It was just after 11.00.

'An early Merry Christmas?' I guessed.

Richard jumped to answer it and we could hear his voice from the kitchen. 'Yes, Sir. Of course. He's right here. I'll pass the message straight on to him.'

The phone tinged down, and Richard poked his nose cautiously around the door.

'It was his Lordship, Dad. He walked across the show paddock this afternoon, and he says there are a lot of stones . . .'

Farming Press

Below is a sample of the wide range of agricultural and veterinary books and videos we publish. For more information or for a free illustrated catalogue of all our publications please contact:

Farming Press Books & Videos
Miller Freeman Professional Ltd
2 Wharfedale Road, Ipswich IP1 4LG, United Kingdom
Telephone (01473) 241122   Fax (01473) 240501

They All Ran After the Farmer's Wife
Veronica Frater

The true story of a farmer's wife coping with seven young children, bed and breakfast and holiday cottage lets.

Summer Holidaze   Veronica Frater

Veronica battles humorously through the summer with her horde of children off school and the holiday lettings in full spate.

Buttercup Jill   Peggy Grayson

Amusing and entertaining memories of a pre-war rural childhood. Full of lively dogs, unpredictable horses and eccentric country characters.

One Dog, His Man & His Trials   Marjorie Quarton

Shep's tales of a sheepdog's life in Ireland with its rogues, adventures and humorous encounters, canine and human.

The Hired Lad   Ian Thomson

A young man's first work on a Scottish farm when horses were yielding to tractor and bothy life was rough and ready.

Falling For It   Geoff Surtees

Geoff Surtees looks back to when, as a wide-eyed teenager, he took his first job as a forester on a Northumbrian estate, recalling the characters, wildlife and the time when the woods echoed to the sound of axes rather than chainsaws.

The Spacious Days   Michael Twist

Growing up on a Buckinghamshire estate in the 1930s. Anecdotes about the farm staff, agricultural work, gamekeeping and the countryside.

Early to Rise   Hugh Barrett

An authentic and highly praised account of life as a farm pupil in the early 1930s.

Farming Press Books & Videos is a division of Miller Freeman Professional Ltd which provides a wide range of media services in agriculture and allied businesses. Among the magazines published by the group are Arable Farming, Dairy Farmer, Farming News, Pig Farming, *and* What's New in Farming. *For a specimen copy of any of these please contact the address above.*